Freaky Fashions

Caroline Archer

Illustrated by
Sara Sliwinska and
Carol Tarrant

BEAVER BOOKS

A Beaver Book
Published by Arrow Books Limited
62–5 Chandos Place, London WC2N 4NW

An imprint of Century Hutchinson Ltd

London Melbourne Sydney Auckland
Johannesburg and agencies throughout the world

First published 1987

Text © Victorama Ltd 1987
Illustrations © Century Hutchinson Ltd 1987

Set in Baskerville
by JH Graphics Ltd, Reading

Made and printed in Great Britain
by Anchor Brendon Ltd
Tiptree, Essex

ISBN 0 09 947210 4

Contents

Introduction

Fashion is fun. It's fun to look at, fun to read about and fun to wear. And it's even more fun if, instead of following it slavishly and looking like everybody else, you create your own look and your own style.

Freaky Fashions has been written to show how, with a certain amount of time, a little ingenuity and the minimum of skill, you can create highly individual and stunning effects at very little cost. It points out useful buys, shows how existing clothes can be transformed, and how old, seemingly useless ones can be turned into exciting and original creations. It has been written primarily for girls, but most of the suggestions can be used on boys' clothes too.

Certain sewing and craft techniques are mentioned in the text, and described in detail in Chapter 5. Instructions for making actual garments are beyond the scope of this book — it is simply intended to give you ideas and show how they can be carried out. It looks at the changing face of fashion in the twentieth century, at how to create six individual 'looks', at clever ways of turning ordinary clothes into something special, and of creating amazing accessories. Finally, no book on fashion is complete without a look at make-up and hairstyles, so these have been included in Chapters 6 and 7.

Treat the ideas in the book as you would a new fashion. Adopt them if they're right for you, adapt them if you know how they would suit you better, discard them and try something else if you don't like them. Above all, have fun.

The 1900s Look

1. What is fashion?

Fashions, along with most other aspects of our everyday lives, have changed dramatically and at an ever-increasing pace this century. In 1900 women wore long skirts, for to reveal so much as an ankle was considered indecorous. Under the frills and flounces of their magnificent gowns women were clad in long stays, from just under the bust to round the hips, tightly laced to achieve the desired effect of a tiny waist. Pads were fitted under the arms and on the hips to further accentuate the waist, and then there were drawers and petticoats and stockings. It took a long time to dress in those days, and a fashionable lady could not manage the job on her own.

Her hairstyle, too, was a work of art. The mass of hair was plumped out still further by back-combing, pads of horsehair, false pieces of human hair, and many decorative ornaments and combs. On top of this was perched the huge and heavy hat, often decorated with plumes, which had to be firmly fixed in place with long and dangerous-looking hat pins. It is hard for us to imagine being able to do anything but walk slowly or sit down with the head held high when dressed in so exaggerated a style.

For just one part of the day, the tea hour, women were allowed to escape from their rigidly constricting corsets and wear softer, more flowing lines, which must have been a great relief to them.

Gradually, however, clothes for women did become

The 1920s Look

more comfortable and more practical. Rigid corseting went out and figures were allowed to become more natural. During the First World War skirts rose from floor level to just above the ankle, as middle-class women for the first time in history began to work outside the home.

Hemlines continued to rise after the First World War until the complete fashion revolution of the 1920s. In their straight-cut, knee-length dresses, with flattened bosoms and no waists (the dresses were often belted round the hips), Twenties women looked totally different from women in the early years of the century. For the first time in history they cut their hair into short, head-hugging bobs, and this, together with their nursery-style strap shoes, gave them a little-girl look. The 'ideal woman' became, instead of a curvaceous, matronly, upright figure, a daring, dashing tomboy. Loose baggy trousers also appeared on the scene, adding to women's emancipation, and a fashion designer, Gabrielle Chanel, overturned another convention when she appeared sporting a suntan. Until then fashionable beauties had had porcelain white skins, enlivened by just a touch of colour on the cheeks and lips (achieved by pinching them with the fingers, for make-up had been taboo). But both men and women followed Chanel's lead, and tanning became the in thing. Make-up gradually came to be accepted too, though the older generation considered it very 'fast'.

The fun and freedom of the 1920s was brought to an end by the Wall Street stock market crash of 1929 and the economic depression that followed. The gay, bright fashions of the Twenties looked out of place in the harsh seriousness of the Thirties, and clothes became more adult-looking, more severe, and were worn in darker colours. The idealized woman looked mature and

The 1930s Look

sophisticated, and wore practical, square-shouldered dresses by day and elegant, slinky dresses at night.

The Second World War naturally had a great influence over Forties fashions. Fabrics were in short supply, and women had to have practical clothes, as many of

The 1940s Look

them were working in factories and on the land to keep the country going during wartime. Trousers were worn for warmth rather than glamour, skirts were short for ease of movement, colours were sombre in accordance with the times. But in 1947, two years after the war

Dior's New Look
c. 1947

had ended, this utilitarian approach to fashion was over-thrown when Christian Dior introduced his New Look. He created dresses with lavish skirts, long and full, tightly gathered at the top into a tiny waist that again thrust women back into corsets if they wanted to be in fashion. After the wartime austerity the look was welcomed as being ultra-feminine and glamorous, and its shape led the way into the Fifties.

Since the 1920s fashion had been influenced by the movies – Clara Bow in the Twenties, Jean Harlow and Greta Garbo in the Thirties, Rita Hayworth and Jane Russell in the Forties – but in the Fifties a new star appeared who had perhaps the greatest influence on fashion of any of them, Marilyn Monroe. Her tight sweaters and famous wiggle encouraged women to wear padded uplift bras to enhance their bosoms, and tight, 'pencil-slim' skirts with high-heeled shoes, which made it impossible to walk any other way than with a wiggle. The Fifties, too, saw the birth of the 'teenager', for until then, though teenagers had, of course, existed, they had had no influence on fashion or on anything else. But thanks to their recognition, Fifties fashion began to include casual clothes as well as the glamorous, 'adult' ones of earlier years. Tapered-leg trousers were worn with flat shoes and overshirts, hair was often taken up into a pony tail with a short fringe, and the whole look was modelled on American teenage high school kids.

But although casual clothes became fashionable, it was not until the Sixties and Seventies that styles really relaxed and fashion became more of a matter of individual choice. The mini-skirt – at first four inches above the knee – was introduced in 1964 by André Courrèges, and by the end of the decade had become so short that bending over revealed the wearer's knickers. Yet the mini-skirt was counterbalanced by the

The First Mini-skirt by Courrèges c. 1964

'granny' look. Girls wore long, ankle- or floor-length dresses and shawls, put their hair up in a bun and often wore little round 'granny specs' to complete the picture.

Hairstyles changed a lot in this period, too, and became more important. In the late Fifties and early

Sixties women began to set their hair in rollers and comb it out into bouffant hairdos — the most exaggerated of which were back-combed and lacquered until they became almost independent creations — hair, as one stylist advised, that should be dusted rather than brushed. The bouffant was succeeded by Vidal Sassoon's straight, sleek haircuts that depended on cut, not setting, for their effect. Many girls grew their hair long and wore it straight and loose, to emphasize the natural look. And this style in turn was counterbalanced by the permed, frizzed-out look, which also became popular in the Seventies.

It was in the Sixties that blue jeans came into fashion, leading to denim garments of all kinds. On several occasions in the last twenty years or so fashion writers have pronounced that jeans are 'dead' and that soon no one will be wearing them. But every time this happens they appear again and seem likely to be around for ever, probably because they are so comfortable.

The last two decades also saw the fashions for second-hand clothes, and for 'dressing in costume'. Instead of simply following a fashion people began to dress a part, so they could be seen in frilly mini-dresses looking like toddlers, in jeans and tan leather boots like cowboys, in long dresses like grannies, in a pastiche of Thirties elegance, and many other 'costumes'. This has led the way into the Eighties, a part of which is still costume dressed, for example, the punk look.

And so today fashion still says that you can do your own thing and create your own look. But it may not last. Fashion writers tell us that the classic look — neat, tidy, well-cut clothes — is on the way back. Who knows what you may be wearing in ten years' time? But that is the fun of the whole fashion game.

2. How to create a 'look'

If fashion in the 1980s means creating your own look, how do you go about it? The first thing to do is to decide which look you want to achieve. It is very easy when you see clothes that appeal to you, to buy or make a bit of this and a bit of that and then discover when you wear the clothes that nothing looks right. If you want to look stylish, you have to put a bit of effort into it.

First of all study the kinds of clothes that are around. Look in the shops (there's no need to buy), look in magazines, see what people in the street are wearing. Make a note of the kind of look that appeals to you and try and analyze what goes into creating it. When you have a list of most of the items, look through your own clothes to see which garments are right for the look and which can be adapted before you start spending money or asking your parents for new clothes. And don't discard those things that don't seem right at this stage, for in a few months' time you may change your mind and want to create something completely different. Or you may want to create several different looks now, so that on some days you can be one kind of person and on others another. You don't necessarily have to stick to one thing!

There are lots of different looks, and it is difficult to separate them completely, because some of them overlap. But for the sake of definition, they have been divided here into the following: the sporty look, the punk look, the exotic look, the zany look, the romantic look, and the unisex look.

THE SPORTY LOOK

The sporty look first sprang up as a result of the popularity of American casual clothes in the mid-Fifties. The look spread to Europe where it became more elegant, and casual clothes became high fashion and commanded very high prices. But the influence of this kind of clothing was so great that it became available in almost every price range, as a look round any of the cheaper popular clothing stores shows.

If this is the look for you then it is quite easy to achieve. Look out for the kind of jacket and trousers you would like in the expensive shops, then check the cheaper ones to see which has the nearest equivalent. Beat the label collectors at their own game by designing your own, and sewing them into your clothes. If your friends go for Italian-style clothes, make labels saying 'Carolani, Milano' for example, if your name is Carol. This gives a nice, joky element to your clothes, and if your friends don't appreciate it then tell them they are snobs!

The kind of shop that sells government surplus stock is sometimes a good source of cheap jackets, though you do *not* want the camouflage kind! They also sell plain, cheap sweaters a good deal more cheaply than fashion stores, and these could be jazzed up with mock designer labels or monogrammed with your initials. You may also find cotton drill trousers in this kind of shop, and again, they will be a great deal cheaper than in

The Sporty Look
(Winter left and
Summer right)

the average fashion clothes shop.

T-shirts and shirts can be extremely expensive in some places and very cheap in others, so again look around very carefully before you buy. Sometimes men's or boys' shirts are a better bet than girls' shirt-type blouses. If they are rather large, so much the better. You can roll up the sleeves and knot the lower part round your waist, or leave the shirt hanging out and belt it with a leather belt, or a man's tie, or a length of webbing or cord.

The kind of ski pant trousers that have straps under the feet to keep them stretched have become popular again. See if you can raid a relative's wardrobe in case they had some years ago and haven't thrown them out. They may even have a pair of pointed-toe ankle boots to go with them, if you are lucky.

On your feet wear plimsolls or trainers, and if you want to look smart, keep them clean. Filthy old shoes do not look sporty! In winter you really need a good pair of boots, but if leather ones are too expensive, buy canvas ones, or rubber wellington-type boots. These have the advantage of keeping you dry in the rain and snow, and if you buy them large enough you can wear a thick pair of socks underneath to keep your feet warm.

In summer the aim is to look healthy and outdoor, so try if you can to get a suntan. If you spend as much time outdoors as possible you will get some kind of tan, even in a poor English summer. You can cheat by using golden-toned make-up, or even the kind of artificial tanning lotion you rub in, but the latter has to be used with great care if you are to avoid ending up looking streaky. Practise first on your tummy or some other hidden part of your anatomy until you are sure you've got the technique right.

Longish, loose-legged shorts are very fashionable in

summer, but if you can't afford any you could cut down an old pair of culottes.

You can also create the sporty look from real sports clothes. For example, if you have some old tennis gear, or jodhpurs, then wear them as ordinary clothes. You could wear a cotton sweater (with your 'designer' name embroidered on it) over a tennis skirt in summertime, and if your legs are tanned and you are not wearing plimsolls you will look very trendy, and not as if you have just left the municipal tennis courts. Wear your jodhpurs with a pair of ordinary boots, a shirt tied with a scarf round your waist and a casual jacket and you will look fashionable rather than horsy.

The sporty look is helped by having a large topcoat or raincoat that fits over all your other clothes, but these can be expensive to buy unless you can get them second-hand. Sometimes mail order firms sell these kinds of coats more cheaply than shops do, so it's worth keeping an eye open for advertisements. Would-be sporty adults use large, brightly-coloured golf umbrellas to keep the rain off, and one of these would be a great find. Try your local transport lost property office (people are always leaving umbrellas on buses and trains), and if you can't find a golf umbrella try and find a man's black umbrella with a wooden handle – not the black leather kind that executive types carry.

THE PUNK LOOK

If you want to look punk then you have to look outrageous, and this can be difficult if you have to lead an ordinary life, keep your parents happy, and go to school. But there are ways round it. For example, in Chapter 7 on hair, you can see how a nice neat bob or short hair-do can be turned into wonderful punk spikes for a party and then back to the conventional look the next day. This means you don't have to commit yourself to the kind of punk hair-do you just have to live with until it grows out.

Similarly, a punk look can be created by skilful use of make-up. For a special occasion, try red or silver eye shadow, with lots of black round your eyes and face painting done in black or red. There are lots of exciting make-up ideas in Chapter 6.

Old clothes that are no longer worn are a good bet if you want to experiment with a punk look. Tear an old shirt or T-shirt and hold it together with a very large safety pin. Cut the sleeves off a faded old T-shirt to make a punk vest. Try splodging it with fabric dye or indelible ink to give it an interesting look (see Chapter 5 for information about dyeing).

Jeans can be made skin tight in the good old way your parents may have tried, that is, by wearing them in the bath to shrink them to your shape. It's a fairly uncomfortable business but we all have to suffer in the interests of fashion! It doesn't work on all jeans, either; some are pre-shrunk, so check the label before you plunge in.

Thick black tights or leggings can be worn with a very short mini-skirt over the top, and a heavy belt slung round the hips. Punk-look belts can, of course, be bought, but the heavier ones, well studded with metal, are very expensive. If you are small and slim you could try buying one or more dogs' choker chains from a pet shop – cheaper than buying belts. But you have to be small enough to be able to wriggle into them, so they are not for the well-built! What you do is simply hold the ring at one end and 'pour' the chain through it to make a loop, which you then pull up over your hips.

The Punk Look

Then when you've got the chain the required length, simply tie it in place with a piece of fuse wire or a black ribbon.

If you want to wear trousers and boots and can't afford proper leather boots then buy canvas lace-up ones instead. The whole look is completed with a studded leather jacket, but these too are very expensive. You could try to buy a motor-bike jacket secondhand, or maybe even borrow one from a kind older friend for a special occasion. Failing that, keep your punk look for warm summer weather when a jacket would be too uncomfortable to wear even if you had one.

THE EXOTIC LOOK

If the exotic look is what you crave then it means you have a longing for the dramatic, and perhaps would like to see yourself as an actress. For the exotic look means looking like an eastern princess, an exiled Russian aristocrat, a gipsy, or a fiery Latin dancer. To achieve these effects you need to wear deep, rich, mysterious colours – black, bottle green, burgundy, indigo, purple, chestnut, or bright reds and oranges if you favour the Latin look. The look tends to be easier to achieve if you are dark rather than fair, but if you have fair hair which stops you looking like a gipsy, you can always bind it up in a swathe of richly patterned and coloured material to make a kind of turban.

For the eastern princess or gipsy look you need long, flowing skirts in rich colours (the cotton Indian ones are ideal), pretty blouses rather than shirts, and lots of beads and jewellery. You can wear large round ear-rings, beads and bangles – *lots* of bangles if you have them. A fringed shawl would complete the look, and

The Gipsy Look

these are best found in secondhand shops, markets and jumble sales. Or a large head square would do, worn as a shawl. An old lace-trimmed petticoat to show below the skirt would be just right. If you don't have one you could cheat and buy some cheap lace trimming from a haberdasher's and sew it on the hem of your skirt. On your feet, wear thonged sandals in summer and high boots in winter.

For the Russian aristocrat look you can wear similar clothes but not patterned flowing skirts and blouses. Look out for satin blouses in red or purple and wear them with a dark but toning skirt. Shawls would be OK here, but they would need to be of the more expensive wool variety – the kind of thing women wore round their shoulders over their winter coats a few years ago. You might find a discarded one in a jumble sale. The ideal to complete this look would be a maxi-coat of the kind that was fashionable in the early 1970s, and if you can find one of these you should have no trouble in achieving the look.

If you want to wear trousers instead of skirts then don't choose the active, sporty-looking kind. Go for the sort that look as if they would spend the day on a chaise longue while their wearer ate Turkish Delight and sipped sherbet – baggy harem pants, tight at the ankle and billowing above, or baggy cossack trousers tucked into high boots. In summer you could also wear loose, flowing, pyjama-type garments (which may well be real pyjamas – though not the striped sort) or long, flowing dresses, though not the Laura Ashley type.

Accessories to go with this look include long scarves, tied round your neck and left to float in the breeze, decorated waistcoats to go over either pretty white blouses or deep-coloured ones, and richly coloured tights to match your skirt.

The Latin Dancer Look

If you have long hair then either leave it flowing loose or put it up in a sophisticated style. If you put it up you could wear exotic-looking combs in it, in colours to match your clothes.

For the Latin dancer look try and get hold of a red

dress with a low front and a tiered, frilled skirt. You could cheat and sew frills on to an ordinary dress if you like. Sweep your hair round to one side of your face, and at the other side pin a large red flower, which you can either buy, pick or make. Olé, you will have transformed yourself into a Spanish señorita.

THE ZANY LOOK

If your aim is to look jolly and amusing, then you have the most choice and can have the most fun out of all the looks, for it means dressing with a sense of humour. The 'Annie Hall' look of the late Seventies was zany, and so too is the punk look if not carried to extremes, but there are lots of others.

The zany look, above all, means wearing bright, happy colours – the best example is yellow. Yellow goes well with bright green and white, and stripes and spots go well with it too. Bright yellow trousers, for example, worn with a green and white striped top would look very cheerful.

However, there is more to the zany look than wearing cheerful colours. You have to look around for clothes and accessories that have a sense of humour in themselves.

Animal motifs often lend themselves well to the zany look, and you can often buy sew- or iron-on motifs for sweaters, T-shirts, bags, and so on. Frogs, hippos, cows, ducks, cats and puppies are all popular motifs, and you could make some yourself and sew them on (see Chapter 5 on crafts). You can also buy sweaters and other clothes with motifs already in place, so maybe you could drop a few hints at Christmas or birthday times!

The other kind of decoration that goes very well with

the zany look is what artists call *trompe l'oeil*, which is French for 'deceiving the eye' and means just that — something that looks like something it isn't. For example, you can buy splendidly jokey jumpers that look as if they have a bow tie round the neck and a handkerchief coming out of a pocket — but in fact it is just part of the knitting pattern. This effect was first achieved in 1920s with a sweater which looked as if it had a large floppy scarf tied in a bow round the neck, so it is not new but can be great fun. If you can knit you could make yourself a *trompe l'oeil* jumper, or you could embroider an existing jumper. What about a ladybird crawling up the sleeve, or a large black spider? That would give your friends a shock!

For the zany look in summer try wearing a mini-skirt over striped leggings and a striped T-shirt, and wear a hat with a silly flower in it. One way to make a really silly flower is to twist a piece of green garden wire round the hat and leave about 30 cm (1 ft) over, to which you attach a cardboard daisy (the larger and more absurd-looking the better). As you walk, the wire and the daisy will wave stupidly up and down, to give a very amusing effect. Wear a T-shirt with a brightly-coloured tie, or a collarless 'grandad' shirt with a tie.

Brightly coloured shoes are another key to a zany look, so, if you can, buy cheap canvas shoes in pink, green or yellow, or dye your existing ones. If you have two pairs of old, brightly coloured tights in different colours, cut one leg off each and wear them both, so you end up with one pink leg and one green leg. You can also wear bright socks over bright tights — and the socks could be odd, too, to create a riot of colour!

There are lots of super, cheap, zany accessories in the shops to help the look along. Bright hair clips and ornaments such as butterfly clips can be pinned on to clothes as well as hair, enormous dangly plastic earrings can be fun, fingerless gloves in vivid colours look terrific, and you can both make and buy zany jewellery. What about stringing little sweets on to earrings, or on wire to make a necklace?

When winter comes wear lots of layers of zany clothes. Top several layers of shirts and sweaters with a really enormous sweater tied round the waist with an old tie, or with a piece of braid or a bright piece of ribbon. If you can afford it buy colourful ankle-high suede boots and wear them with striped leg warmers, or snazzy tights or leggings and a pair of socks, too, if it is cold. Long, striped knitted scarves look fun and are very easy to make — see Chapter 5 on crafts. For winter, too, you could dye an old vest and wear it *over* your clothes to convince everyone you are 'wrapping up warm for winter'. In fact, for the zany look, you can really go to town on tie-and-dye and other crafts, again see Chapter 5.

A final thought about hair. If yours is long enough, plait it and wind pieces of wire through the plaits, then curve the wire out so you look like a cartoon naughty schoolgirl. That should give everyone a good laugh!

THE ROMANTIC LOOK

At some time or other in her life even the most tomboyish girl longs to look romantic. She may spend most of her time dressed in jeans and a T-shirt yet still dream of seeing herself in a delicate ballgown with layers of white tulle billowing gently about her. Real life isn't like that for most of us, but we can still indulge our romantic fantasies a little.

It is easier to put together a romantic look in summer

because cotton dresses in pastel colours and pretty prints lend themselves to it so well. Flower-sprigged fabrics of the Laura Ashley type are ideal for this look, together with plain fabrics in soft pale pink, cream, blue, green or light coffee colours. For summer, white is always good, too. Skirts and dresses need to be fairly long, though for sundresses they can have low-cut necklines or backs. But, generally speaking, looking romantic means looking back into the past when women wore long dresses and covered up their bodies rather than revealing them.

Buy a white, lace-trimmed petticoat from a junk shop and wear it as a skirt, or wear it peeping out from under another skirt. You could make a lace skirt quite cheaply from cotton lace curtain material, and wear it over white tights. Any clothes trimmed with frills or lace or broderie anglaise are ideal for the romantic look, and you can quite easily convert an existing dress or blouse by sewing on these trimmings.

Complete your summer romantic look with a large straw hat trimmed with ribbon and real flowers for a special occasion. Tie a long, floating scarf round your neck, but be careful it doesn't catch in anything. Make an Edwardian velvet choker trimmed with a brooch at the front, and look out for romantic old jewellery, like cameo brooches and pieces set with semi-precious stones. These need not cost a great deal if you look for them in the right places.

Ideally, for the romantic look, you should have long hair, which you can wear loose with the top part taken back in a ribbon, or put up and decorated with pretty combs or flowers. Leave a few tendrils free to escape to soften the look.

In winter wear high-necked blouses with a brooch at the throat, and longish dark-coloured skirts with

The Romantic Look

matching tights. A shawl round the shoulders would keep you warm. The little pointed-toe Victorian-style boots would go very well with this look.

If you want to wear trousers then you will have to opt for a male romantic look rather than a female one – velvet trousers and a velvet jacket, a silky blouse with a large floppy collar, and a scarf tied loosely round the neck in a large bow.

Over the top of these romantic clothes the ideal thing would be a large cloak to wrap around yourself. If you are lucky you just might come across one at a jumble sale.

It's also worth paying attention to detail. You can't look romantic if your hair needs washing and your shoes are filthy! If you have ever been given pretty lace-trimmed hankies at Christmas, then use them. White lace gloves would look good in summer, and patterned leather or mock leather ones would look better than wool in winter. In winter, too, you could have fun wearing hats – largish, floppy-brimmed ones held on with a hat-pin if necessary.

THE UNISEX LOOK

This is the absolute opposite of the romantic look, for real unisex means jeans, shirts, flat shoes and cropped hair with no make-up. It is practical and comfortable and usually adopted by those who think that fashion is frivolous and silly, and that women should not dress themselves up to look attractive for men. For those not committed to these causes it can seem rather dull and not much fun. But there are times when everyone just wants to feel comfortable, and it is a very practical way to dress for doing physical work, like painting your

room, tidying up the garden, going out for walks, and so on.

To make a change from jeans you could wear boiler suits or dungarees over a shirt, T-shirt or sweater. Boys' shirts are better than girls' for this look. They are made wider and longer, and are therefore easier to move freely inside, and they stay tucked into your jeans when you bend over. Incidentally, jeans with this kind of look should never be worn tight or they draw attention to the fact that you are female rather than making you look unisex, especially if you are not too slim.

Sensible lace-up shoes may not look exciting but they are often very comfortable and ideal if you are on your feet all day or doing a lot of walking. They can be worn with woolly socks in the winter and cotton ones in the summer, and if you want to jazz up the look a bit you can wear brightly coloured socks. Boots, of course, can be worn in winter and sandals in summer.

Your haircut should be short and unfussy. You can always zap up this kind of style with colour streaks, gelled curls or spikes from time to time if you want to. And you shouldn't wear any make-up, though a little mascara and lip gloss would be permissible.

This chapter has given you six different 'looks' to aim at, according to the kind of person you are and what your likes and dislikes are. But you may say that you don't want to turn yourself into any of these types. Perhaps one day you'd like to look zany, one day punk and one day unisex. Well, why not? Lots of clothes will fit with one look as well as another if you change the way you wear them and change the accessories you wear with them. A boy's shirt, for example, could be worn as it is tucked into jeans for a unisex look, worn over trousers with a leather belt over it and a scarf round the neck to give a sporty look, or tied in a knot round the waist with a giant-sized plastic brooch pinned to it to give a zany look. That's the whole point about fashion — you should enjoy it, and it should be fun.

3. Clever clothes

In this chapter we will look at individual items of clothing to see how, with a little ingenuity, they can be turned into fantastically fashionable garments with the minimum of cost.

T-SHIRTS

T-shirts are wonderful garments as they can be bought cheaply in all shapes and sizes and worn in lots of different ways. It is fun to have lots of T-shirts in different colours and shapes, but if you can't afford that then try to have at least one enormous one. This can be tucked into a skirt or trousers, worn as a dress loose or belted, worn over a bikini on the beach when it gets chilly or when you've had enough sun, or worn as a nightie.

Although T-shirts are basically cheap you will find that some shops charge a lot more than others, so have a good look around before you buy anything.

Ordinary sized T-shirts are great to keep you warm in winter if worn under a dress or a shirt, or they can be worn like a sweater over a shirt. Sleeveless T-shirts can become vests or waistcoats, as well as useful things to wear on a warm day. Men's vests can be bought as sleeveless T-shirts and dyed or tie-dyed.

T-shirts lend themselves very well to dyeing, tie-dyeing, using as a base for appliqué or embroidery, or for printing messages on (all these techniques are described in detail in Chapter 5).

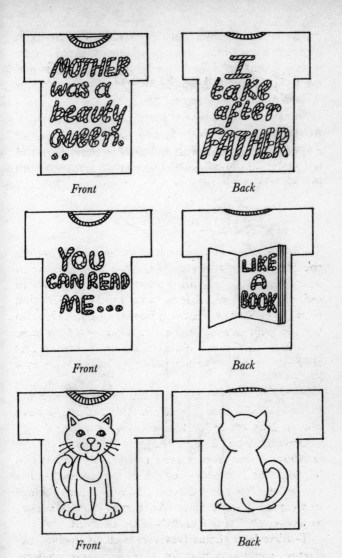

Front   *Back*

Front   *Back*

Front   *Back*

Some zany ideas for livening up T-shirts by printing or embroidery

The kind of T-shirt that ties over the shoulders can be decorated with thin strips of brightly coloured ribbon woven round or plaited together with the straps and the loose ends tied in bows. Brooches, badges or hair ornaments can be fixed to the straps too.

Finally, lots of different motifs, such as the simple shapes below, can be made and sewn on to T-shirts. Take care that you cut them out of washable, colourfast material, though, if you don't want the colours to spread everywhere.

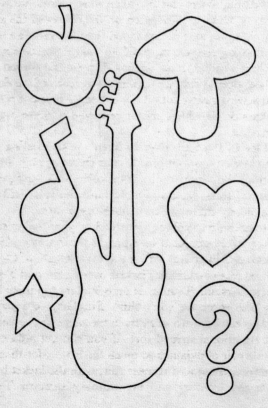

SHIRTS AND BLOUSES

Shirts and blouses too come in lots of different shapes, styles and sizes. As we saw in the previous chapter, you can wear a high-necked frilly blouse and look like an Edwardian lady, or a boy's large shirt and look sporty. But whatever style of shirt or blouse you favour, there are lots of things you can do to make them exciting and unique.

Existing shirts can be given new collars and extra pockets. Choose a variation on the colour of the shirt. For example, if the shirt is red then use red and white spotted or striped material to make the collar and pockets. An old, long-sleeved shirt can be turned into a short-sleeved shirt by cutting off the ends of the sleeves and sewing neatly round the cut edges to make a hem. Collars on old shirts can be removed to make a grandad shirt.

One of the best ways to liven up an existing shirt is to sew on new buttons. If your shirt has plain boring buttons, buy some in the shape of animals, or liquorice allsorts, stars, hearts or bows and the shirt will look completely different and much more fun.

Large shirts, perhaps discarded by your dad or found at a jumble sale, can be worn as mini-dresses, belted round the waist and with the sleeves rolled up. Or they can be worn as summer jackets over a skirt and T-shirt, or trousers and T-shirt, again belted to stop them looking like someone else's shirt. Similarly, old pyjama jackets can be worn as shirts in the same way, especially the traditional striped sort. If you can get hold of the whole pair of pyjamas so much the better, for then you can wear them as a trouser suit, with the jacket belted over the trousers and an ordinary shirt or T-shirt

An old pair of striped pyjamas makes a great new outfit

underneath. Roll the sleeves up to the elbow and the trousers up to mid-calf length, and no one will suspect you are wearing a pair of old pyjamas! If they will not stay rolled up then slipstitch them into place.

If you like pretty, embroidered blouses but their cost deters you from buying one, then embroider your own design on to an existing plain blouse. A soft, romantic look can be created by using pastel colours on a light background, an elegant effect by embroidering a slightly lighter or darker colour than the background. A pale coffee colour on a cream, silky blouse would look very smart.

If, however, you want to look bright and bold then choose a large image and embroider it in a vivid colour or colours. The only problem with this is that it will take you longer to complete the effect!

It's fun to wear a tie with a shirt-type blouse. This can be a proper tie tied with a proper knot, or can simply be a length of material or ribbon, either tied in the same way or as a loose bow.

An old shirt made of heavyish material can be turned into a waistcoat by cutting off the sleeves and hemming in the loose edges thus formed. This can then be worn over another shirt, a sweater, or a T-shirt, and would look good with either a skirt or with trousers.

SWEATERS

If you can knit then you have no excuse for not wearing exciting sweaters. For nowadays patterns can be bought in the most imaginative designs, and many of them do not require a great deal of expertise to make them up. Even if you can only do plain knitting, an attractive sweater can be made very quickly using large needles and chunky wool or mohair in an exciting colour. Mohair has the advantage that its texture can hide small errors, as well as being wonderfully warm and glamorous to wear.

If you do not have the time to knit a new sweater, then there are lots of ways in which you can adapt or brighten up an old one. One of the easiest and quickest is to embroider a message in wool of a contrasting colour. Write the message on the sweater first in chalk and then embroider it in stem stitch or chain stitch (see pages 91–3). You need a large, blunt-ended darning needle to sew with wool. Choose wool of a similar thickness to the sweater for your message, which can be anything from a bold 'I'm the greatest' to the name of your school or college. Of course, the embroidery need not take the form of a message. You could embroider a design. For example, on the front you might 'draw' a cat, and then take its tail all the way round the back to appear at the front again. Or you could sew the outline of a sheep, and then make its wool from little loops of real wool, secured by small stitches on the wrong side. Lots of animals can be embroidered on using this technique. For example, a lion could have a real mane hanging from its neck, or a pony a mane and a tail. It makes the jumper a bit more difficult to handle in the wash, but provided you are careful no harm should come to it.

Of course a motif or message does not have to be embroidered on. The appliqué technique, as suggested for T-shirts and described in detail on pages 100–102, can be used just as well on sweaters, but again, unless you have all your jumpers dry-cleaned you will have to make sure that whatever material you use will not run in the wash.

A really large man's sweater can look great with the

I'm the
GREATEST

PRETENTIOUS
– moi?

THINK AHEAD
aha!

Fun messages to embroider on sweaters

sleeves pushed up and with a wide belt to make it into a mini-dress.

If you are in the habit of leaning on your elbows all the time and have worn holes in your sleeves, you can patch them with denim from a pair of old jeans, or with a piece of brightly patterned material. Or you could simply unpick the sleeve seam, bind the edge with tape and wear the sweater as a waistcoat. But you have to take care not to cut through any stitches when doing this or the whole jumper may unravel!

Under a jacket a cardigan will double as a sweater if worn back to front, and there are other effective ways of cheating, too. False polo necks can be either knitted or bought and worn inside a round- or V-necked jumper. They have the advantage of keeping you warm as well as making the jumper look different! You can knit small squares in a contrasting colour with a stripe of the main sweater colour and sew them on an existing sweater as pockets. A scarf is very easy to knit and makes a plain sweater look more exciting. If you get tired of it flopping about you could sew it lightly in place, or pin it with a badge or brooch. A false fringe can be added to the welt of an existing jumper to make it look different, and, of course, to disguise the fact that it is a bit too short!

Finally, and if you are prepared to put in a bit more work, you can have a lot of fun creating a *trompe l'oeil* effect. For example, you could carefully and cunningly embroider on your sweater a necklace, with real beads sewn on to it, which would look as if you were really wearing a separate necklace. Many of the amusing designer sweaters that can be bought nowadays create this kind of effect — a bow tie, a pocket handkerchief, a shirt front and tie — and they can all be added afterwards rather than knitted in if you are prepared to take

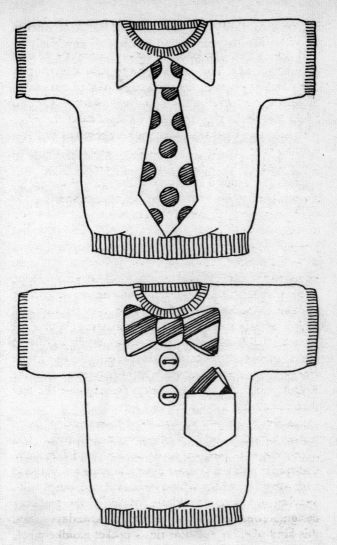

The collar, tie, bow tie and handkerchief can all be embroidered on existing sweaters

the time to do it. You will need to use neat stitches in a contrasting colour and be sure to cover all the existing sweater colour, so it takes time. A white bow tie, for example, could be embroidered, using satin stitch, on a black or navy jumper. You would have to draw it on first using chalk and then carefully fill in your outline. You could leave round dots to make a navy-spotted tie, or embroider them in with red to make a red-spotted tie. A long tie could be made in a similar way, though it would take longer to do. But if you were really ambitious you could create a stunning effect by making a patterned tie in exciting colours.

TROUSERS

Trousers are more difficult to adapt and decorate than T-shirts, blouses and jumpers. This is because their shape is vital to the way they fit and the effect they create, and if you start to try and change the shape then you may well end up with a pair of unwearable trousers. There are, however, some things you can do.

One is to cut the bottoms off a pair of long trousers to turn them into the fashionable mid-calf length. Cotton trousers or jeans can be tie-dyed using a bleach solution instead of a dye to create interesting patterns on them. If you do use bleach take great care when handling it, for if you splash it on your skin it will burn, and if you splash it on your clothing it will bleach areas you don't want bleached! If you do get any on your skin then rinse it off at once with cold water. Clothing tie-dyed with bleach must be thoroughly rinsed while still tied up or the bleach will run all over the fabric and ruin the pattern you are trying to create.

If you like wearing track suits and leisure suits then

you can acquire one in whatever colour you like, very cheaply, by buying men's knitted cotton long johns and dyeing them. You will sometimes find these on market stalls for a few pounds. The tops could also be worn separately as T-shirts, and the bottoms can be worn as leggings under skirts. Or the whole outfit can simply be worn as it was intended – under trousers and tops in winter to keep warm – particularly useful if you take part in a lot of outdoor activities in winter, or if your winter trousers are rather thin.

Both cotton and winter-weight trousers can be given braided 'seams' down the outside of the legs or round the bottoms. They can be decorated with motifs stitched on to pockets.

If you want to create something exciting for evening wear then you could sew sequins on to your trousers, either in rows to create stripes, or in patterns. Sequinned knee patches would be an amusing touch, or if you want to be more conventional, you could sew on sequinned flowers or geometric patterns.

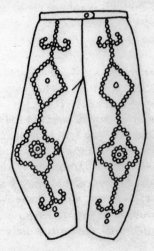

Sequins look stunning sewn on trousers for evening wear

The appearance of a pair of trousers can be changed dramatically by wearing an unusual belt. You will find more about belts in Chapter 4. Or you could make an amusing pair of braces out of coloured broad elastic and wear these to hold up your trousers.

Trousers can also be cut down to make shorts. If you are going to do this, try them on first and measure how long you think you would like the shorts to be, then leave a good 15 cm (6 in) or so extra when you cut the material just in case you change your mind. If you want your shorts to have turn-ups then don't forget to take these into your calculations too.

Longish, loose, patterned shorts are now very fashionable. You could scrounge a pair of old school shorts of the divided-skirt type and decorate them by tie-dyeing (or bleaching) or potato printing. Or an old pair of culottes could be cut down and treated in a similar way. If you have an old pair of shorts that nowadays look too short, then you could sew false bottoms on them as turn-ups, or just use braid of a contrasting colour and sew some up the seams, too, so it doesn't look like an afterthought.

SKIRTS

Skirts, especially summer ones, are a lot easier to make, adapt and change than trousers are. You can make a skirt from a length of fabric wrapped round your waist and hips and knotted at the top, without any sewing at all. You can wear a long skirt or a short one, a tight one or a full one, whatever takes your fancy, and easily make one by cutting down a dress you no longer care for. Conversely, a loose, gathered skirt with an elasticated waistband can be turned into a summer sundress by pulling the waistband up to just under the armpits and tying a ribbon round the waist. If you feel insecure you could make thin straps of ribbon as shoulder straps to hold it up.

If you want to create an impact, cut the hem of a full skirt into longish ziz-zag points. If you don't want to hem it then iron on a binding tape to stop it from fraying. If you are feeling really daring, sew beads or little bells on the points.

Buy a pretty petticoat and loop up one side of your skirt to show it underneath, as ladies used to do in the eighteenth century. Petticoats can often be worn as skirts in their own right if they are the pretty, cotton, lace- or broderie-anglaise-trimmed sort. Secondhand clothes shops often sell beautiful old petticoats quite cheaply. A Fifties-style, bouffant-shape petticoat can be made by sewing gathered lace in tiers on the underside of the petticoat; it can then be worn either under a light cotton skirt or on its own. If you team up a pretty petticoat with a sleeveless, low-necked cotton top and tie a coloured sash (made out of a length of material) round the waist then you will have an ideal dress for a hot summer's day.

Lace skirts are now very fashionable. You could make one out of old net curtains if you give them a good wash first, and wear it over patterned white tights or leggings. If your curtain is not large enough to make a skirt, then fold it into a triangle like a scarf, and tie it round your waist to fall over one hip over another skirt. A shawl could be knotted and worn in this way, too; and, if it is big enough, it can be knotted round and worn as a skirt in its own right.

Gathered skirts of any length are easy to make because they basically consist of a wide tube gathered

at the top by elastic threaded through a waistband, and they need have no fastenings at all if they are made wide enough to stretch over your hips. They can be decorated with lace or braid. If you sew a piece of lace on the underneath of the skirt hem, leaving it long enough to hang down below the hem, it will look like a petticoat underneath.

Mini-skirts are very easy to make, as they require only a small amount of material and little sewing. They can also be made from a longer skirt cut down to size. If you do this, save the material left and make it into a scarf or sash to be worn with the mini-skirt or with a different outfit.

A straight skirt for winter can be made out of a straight piece of knitting, with just one seam up the back and an elasticated waist, which can be hidden with a broad leather belt.

Skirts can be decorated with a wide range of embroidery or appliqué motifs. It is very easy to make patch pockets of a contrasting fabric and sew them on, or, like trousers, skirts can be given coloured braces to hold them up. Different kinds of belts can be worn with them to change their effect. These are described more fully in the next chapter.

Knitted 'tube' skirt

DRESSES

One of the easiest ways of making a dress look different is to create a layered look. A sleeveless jacket, possibly belted at the waist to make it look more like part of the dress, is one way of doing this. A shirt worn under the dress with the collar and sleeves showing is another. A dress that fastens down the front could be worn with a T-shirt underneath and the fastening left open to create a third effect. In winter, a polo-neck jumper could be worn instead of the shirt or T-shirt. In summer, a sundress could be worn over a shirt-type dress, or a large T-shirt could be worn over a dress and belted at the waist.

As with skirts, different effects can be created by wearing different kinds of belts. A scarf or shawl can be worn round the hips, a longer petticoat worn to show underneath, or the skirt of the dress can be caught up at one side to reveal the petticoat underneath. Embroidery or appliqué motifs can be used, extra pockets sewn on, or braid can be added.

It is fun to make a frill to sew on the hem of a dress. If your dress is patterned, then choose one of the colours in the pattern to make your frill. You could add new buttons in the same colour, or Fergie-type bows on the sleeves or bodice.

A large T-shirt or sweater or a short mini-dress looks terrific over matching thick tights or leggings in winter. Add a bow in your hair for decoration. A tunic-style dress also looks good worn in this way over a polo-neck sweater and thick tights. The sweater and tights should match each other, and can either match or contrast with the dress.

For cold winter days a granny-type shawl can look

terrific over a dress and will keep you cosy. A thick woolly scarf will have the same effect, but will look more sporty than a shawl.

For summer wear a dress can be created, without sewing, from a length of material. Start at the back

A dress made from a length of fabric without any sewing required

of your waist, bring it up and over one shoulder, then hold it at waist level while you take the fabric round your waist. Secure it by tucking in the end firmly, and, if you still don't feel safe, by fixing it with a large brooch at the waist at front and back. Take care that the brooches cannot easily come undone and stick into you, though, for that could be very uncomfortable.

OVERCOATS

A good, warm winter coat can be a very expensive item to buy, as you probably know. If you are going to buy one then it is best to choose something that isn't too trendy, so you can wear it for several years if need be, and dress it up with fashionable accessories. If you can't afford a proper overcoat, then a raincoat worn over the kind of quilted waistcoat sold for outdoor wear makes a good substitute and will keep you dry. Quilted jackets are good and warm, too, but need to be worn over thick trousers or skirts if your nether regions are not to freeze. A duffel coat makes a good, inexpensive, warm top layer — as students have discovered for generations!

SHOES

Because they are so expensive shoes are another item that cause difficulty when it comes to trying to dress as you would like. It would be nice to have lots of pairs of shoes in different colours, to match everything you wear, but unless you have plenty of money it isn't possible. However, a cheap alternative is to dye white canvas shoes in vivid colours such as emerald, fuchsia, sunshine yellow and scarlet to match items of clothing.

If you are careful you can create a pattern on canvas shoes. Use indelible marker pens, being very careful not to get them on anything you don't want to mark. Draw a design lightly in pencil first. You may want

Canvas shoes and laces can be decorated with marker pens or sequins

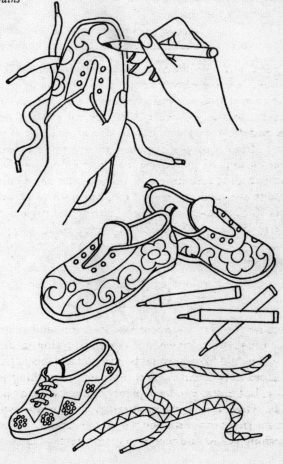

to have swirls of colour, or maybe an amusing landscape with flowers and leaping spring lambs, or a racing car or sailing boat. Start by colouring in the non-adjacent bits and leave them to dry first so the colour doesn't run.

Black canvas shoes could have silver or coloured (or both) sequins stuck on if you want your feet to catch the light in the disco.

If your shoes have laces, buy some in a contrasting colour, or buy white ones and turn them into brilliantly coloured stripes by using indelible marker pens as described above.

BOOTS

Boots are another expensive item to buy. If you can't afford leather ones, then you can console yourself with the knowledge that rubber or plastic ones will keep your feet drier, anyway.

Canvas boots can be treated in the same way as canvas shoes. If you do have an old pair of leather boots that you want to renovate, then use shoe paints rather than dyes. You could create an interesting two-tone effect by, for example, painting the toe caps and heels in a different colour to the main part of the boot.

SANDALS

Cheap flip-flops and plastic sandals can be turned into unique items of footwear by decorating them with hair slides, badges, brooches, artificial, or for a special occasion real flowers, bows, and so on. The kind of sandals that consist of strips of leather or plastic can be decorated with woven ribbons. It would be fun to do the outside of the shoe one colour and the inside

Creating fabulous effects for sandals

another, and then wear them with odd-coloured tights, to create the kind of look that Italian men wore in the Renaissance. Or you could create a striped effect by painting alternate sandal strips with shoe paint.

Gold and silver paint can be sprayed on to plastic sandals, or, for a less permanent effect, little gold stars stuck on to them, to make snazzy shoes for evening.

4. Exciting extras

This chapter looks at all the extra things that go into fashion — socks, tights, hats, belts, bags and so on, which the fashion industry has always lumped together and called accessories. Accessories are fun, because they are cheap to buy and easy to make, and their choice can make your clothes look lively and exciting or formal and serious-minded. Let's start at the top, with head-gear.

HATS

There was a time when no young lady would be seen in public without a hat, and, later, a time when no young lady would be seen dead in one! But at last people have realized that hats can be fun, and have started wearing them again for that reason.

They can also be extremely practical. When there's an icy wind blowing a nice, snug, pull-on hat makes all the difference between misery and comfort. At the opposite end of the temperature spectrum, a hat with a brim to keep the sun off your head and stop you screwing up your eyes when you're trying to read will also be a great boon.

But if you want to wear a hat just for fun, choose one with a brim that you can bend up, down or do whatever you like with. You can pin the brim up with a brooch or a badge, pull the hat well down over your ears to look like a spy or a woman of mystery (or just to keep the rain off), tie a brightly coloured ribbon round the crown to stream in the wind, or, if you're feeling romantic, pin on a flower or two. If you want to make people laugh, make the crazy daisy decoration described on page 31.

You can make a 'universal hat' which is fun for all occasions, and can be used for theatrical purposes, too. All you need is a piece of felt fabric 60 cm (2 ft) square. Your hat will have to be the right size for your head, so it is as well to do a trial run first with an old piece of brown paper. Draw a circle, using a compass, approximately 60 cm (2 ft) in diameter, and inside it, using the same centre, draw another circle approximately 18 cm (7 in) in diameter. (These measurements are based on an adult size and may need adjusting

Making the 'universal hat'

1

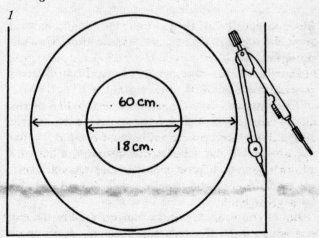

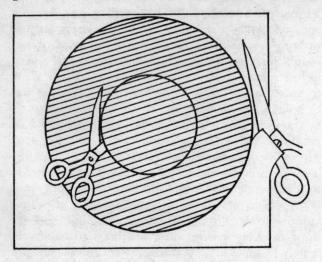

according to how big you are.) Cut round both circles so you are left with a ring — and that is your universal hat. When you've made a brown paper one that seems to fit on your head, then cut out the felt in the same way. Then you can try out some of the things you can do with it.

Put the hat on your head with the 'brim' flopping down and you will look like Greta Garbo. Tilt the brim up in front and you will look like a cowboy. Draw two sides of the felt through the hole in the centre, pull the hat down about your ears, and you will look like Napoleon. Lay the felt flat, lift up one side, draw it towards you then pass it halfway through the hole, giving it a half twist, and you will look like an old-fashioned coal heaver or a fisherman in a sou'wester. This may sound difficult, but once you have the cut-out hat in front of you, you will find the instructions

Some shapes that can be created with the 'universal hat'

easy to follow. You will probably discover lots of other ways of wearing the hat, and will have a great time with it.

Another way to make people laugh with a hat is to make false pigtails and sew them on it. Make them out of several strands of wool plaited together and held by rubber bands at each end. Sew one end of each pigtail to the underside of your hat. If you want them to stick out and look even sillier, weave a piece of wire through each plait and curve it outwards at an angle. Tie a brightly coloured ribbon (odd colours if you like) round the end of each plait in a big bow.

If you want to combine feeling cosy in the depths of winter with looking glamorous, then knit a hat-cum-scarf. This is really a long tube which you pull over your head so one end fits snugly round your neck, under your coat, while the other keeps your head warm. It really works because there aren't any gaps for the wind to whistle through!

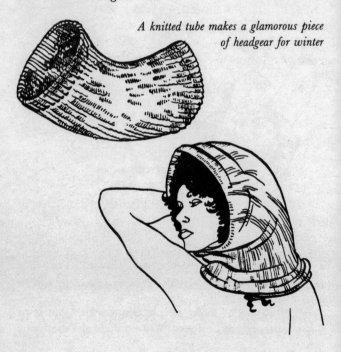

A knitted tube makes a glamorous piece of headgear for winter

SCARVES

Woolly scarves for keeping warm are fun to knit and fun to wear. Make a long narrow one striped in yellow and black; embroider a cat face on one end, make French knitting paws to sew on (see page 99), and you have a tiger scarf — or just a pussy cat, depending on what kind of face you give him. If you are clever enough to knit zig-zag stripes you could have a pet python scarf. If you knit your scarf about 15 cm (6 in) wide and long enough, you can sew up the ends to form little pockets in which you can keep your hands warm.

But scarves can be glamorous as well as practical. Long Indian silk scarves in glowing colours can be bought quite cheaply and have a multitude of uses. They make wonderful sashes for dresses, skirts or trousers; they can be knotted loosely round the neck over a plain sweater, or tied in a flamboyant bow; you can wrap them round your head and then round your neck; you can even use them as headbands and hair ribbons. Large silk or imitation silk squares are also very useful, as they can be used in most of the ways described above but also worn round your shoulders as a shawl, or round your hips over a skirt or trousers.

Small square scarves are handy to knot round your neck, cowboy fashion, or to tie round your hair to keep it out of your eyes on a windy day. You could wear one peeping out of a jacket pocket, like a man's hanky. They are useful, too, for keeping your hair clean if you ever indulge in a spring-cleaning spree or decide to sort through the junk in the attic!

TIES

Ties can, of course, be worn round the neck as intended, but they can also make very useful belts. A striped tie looks good over a plain T-shirt dress, a plain tie could be worn over a patterned dress. Ties can be tied round the tops of skirts or threaded through belt loops on trousers or shorts. They also make good headbands and hair ribbons.

BELTS

Belts are wonderfully versatile. Not only can you make them out of different kinds of materials but you can wear them anywhere from halfway up your chest to low down on your hips.

Instructions are given below for making plaited leather belts but there are lots of other ways of creating an interesting belt. And, of course, you don't have to wear just one at a time – you could take a leaf out of the punks' book and wear several.

You can make a big chunky belt out of twisted rolls of fabric. If you or anyone you know has any longish pieces of fabric left over from either dress- or curtain-making, twist the fabric round and then twist the twist round on itself (rather like a hank of wool). The double twist can then be tied round as a belt.

Long necklaces make good belts, too. You could use bead necklaces, or chains, or a mixture of both. For disco wear, try sequins, which can be bought in bands and either worn as they are or sewn or stuck on to a backing fabric. If you like chain belts you could buy a dog's choker chain (see page 23) and wear that as a belt. You can plait or weave strips of plastic or wool together to make a very colourful belt, or do the same thing with strips of brightly coloured fabric.

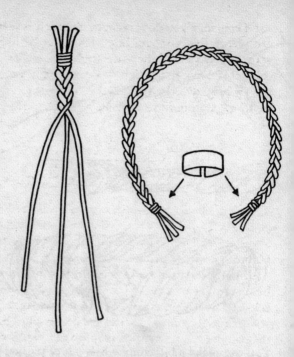

Plaited leather bootlaces make very attractive belts. Leave a few inches to make a fringe at one end and then bind the laces tightly together with thread before you start. Plait until you have almost reached the other end, and bind with thread again. The binding can be covered up with small pieces of leather or leather cloth glued in place.

The haberdashery department of your local store is a good place to look for unusual things from which to make belts. You could try ribbon (either satin finish or velvet), braiding of various kinds, cords of various kinds (from the silk-finish kind used to tie back curtains to the rope-look chunky sort), thickly stranded wools — the variety is almost endless.

Of course, if you don't want to make a belt then there are plenty that you can buy. They can be decorated with shoe paints if they are leather, or with acrylic colours if they are plastic. You could paint on a mock row of brightly coloured 'jewels', or zig-zag stripes, or write an amusing message on a bought belt.

SOCKS, TIGHTS, LEG-WARMERS, ETC.

These are all rather basic things that you need to keep you warm, but as they can nowadays be bought in such a variety of colours and patterns they have become fashion garments in their own right.

Brightly coloured socks are fun, but even these can be made more striking by sewing on sequins, or coloured braid (but make sure this is washable). Tassels sewn on to the backs of socks are fashionable and, like the bobbles on the backs of tennis socks, will stop your socks from sliding down. You can make a tassel by taking a piece of cardboard about 7 cm (3 in) wide by 5

1

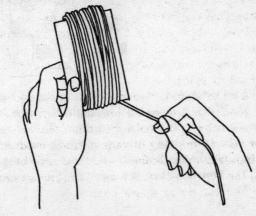

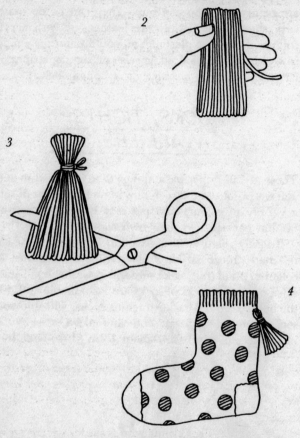

cm (2 in) deep and wrapping knitting cotton round it (see **1**). When it looks thick enough, slide the looped cotton carefully off the cardboard (see **2**). Tie another piece of cotton round the top end, to secure it, then cut through the threads at the bottom to form the tassel (see **3**). You can then sew the tassel on to the sock (see **4**).

Lacy socks look pretty and can be worn over another brightly coloured pair, to create an interesting effect.

Tights are infuriating things as one leg always gets a hole or a ladder in it while the other stays perfect. If this happens with coloured tights, cut the damaged leg off two pairs in contrasting colours and wear them both together, so you have one red leg and one blue leg. They look terrific worn like this, especially if your shoes can be made to tone in with the colour scheme in some way (see page 31). But do make sure that the two pairs worn in this way are of approximately the same thickness. One sheer leg and one thick one would look very peculiar!

Really thick tights can be warmer to wear than trousers in winter so don't be put off and think they are frumpy. In rich red, blue or green, or in patterns, they look very good and a great deal better than blue, pinched legs! At the opposite extreme, very fine, sheer tights with a slight sheen on them, or tights with gold and silver glitter effects, look glamorous with the right kind of dress. They are all great for parties.

Some girls think stockings are more glamorous than tights, but don't forget that you need something with which to hold them up, and suspender belts or garters are pretty uncomfortable to wear, which is why most women were very thankful when tights replaced nylon stockings in the 1960s.

Leg-warmers and leggings are great for winter, worn over ordinary tights or over trousers. Leg-warmers are very easy to knit, as they are just long tubes which can either be knitted on two needles and joined with a seam, or knitted on four needles like socks. Knitting with four needles is not nearly as difficult as it sounds, so don't be put off if you would like to have a go.

GLOVES

After being relegated for years to strictly cold-weather wear, gloves are back in fashion again. Lots of different kinds are on sale — fingerless gloves, lace gloves, gloves in bright, plain colours, striped gloves, fluffy knitted gloves, leather and mock leather gloves—most of which, with the exception of the leather ones, are cheap to buy.

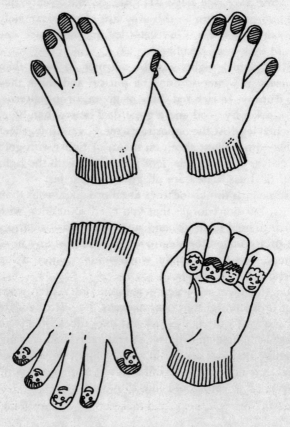

Old fabric gloves can be cheered up by dyeing, or by decorating with bold spots in indelible inks to match your clothes. If they are getting a bit worn at the finger ends then chop the fingers off to make a trendy pair of fingerless gloves.

A pair of plain woollen gloves can be made more amusing by embroidering funny faces on the finger ends. Or you could try embroidering red 'nails' on the ends of the fingers, as a joke. This idea was first introduced by the fashion designer Schiaparelli in the 1920s.

Gloves are difficult things to knit, but if you have a keen knitter in the family perhaps you could persuade them to knit you a boldly striped pair, or a pair with each finger a different colour – though with each hand matching.

Tudor monarchs used to wear rings over their gloves, and you could try this too. Buy big, bold cheap rings, and make sure they are large enough to fit over the fabric.

BAGS

Bags come in all shapes and sizes for all kinds of use – from carrying clothes and belongings for a weekend away to carrying a hanky, a comb and a purse for a party. Some girls seem to need a large bag wherever they go, others prefer to travel light, so if you are setting out to buy a bag consider which type of person you are and for what purpose the bag will chiefly be used before you buy it.

A bag that can either be carried on your shoulder or in your hand is very useful, as is a bag with lots of pockets so you can keep your address book and diary separate from your purse and make-up. If you are going out for a day and possibly bringing back items of shopping, then a light plastic basket is a good idea. The disadvantage of this kind of bag is that your purse can easily be seen in it, which is not a good idea if you are in a crowded place where someone might steal it.

Baskets, either the traditional straw kind or the modern plastic sort, are fun to decorate in your own style. Raffia can be woven into either to make a picture or a motif, or, if you want to look more glamorous, you could use coloured ribbons. Wool could be woven into a design, too, enabling you to create, for example, a pony with a tail made of loose strands of wool hanging down, or a cat with whiskers. Baskets are very good to pin badges on, or to sew motifs on. They can also

Decorating a plastic basket with raffia

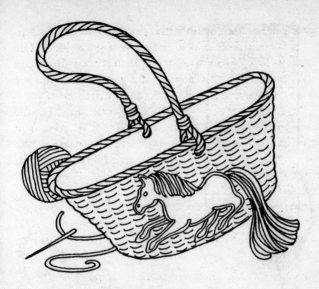

Decorating a straw basket with wool

be decorated with strings of beads, lightly stitched in place.

School satchels (don't shudder!) make good bags. If you can get hold of an old leather one you could paint it with a shoe paint — say pink or pale green — to make a useful and hardwearing bag that doesn't look as if it has anything to do with school.

A simple shoulder bag is very easy to make. You can knit one, or sew one. To make a knitted bag measuring 24 × 25 cm (9½ × 10 in) you will need two 50-gram balls of double knitting wool or mohair, and size 7 needles. Cast on 50 stitches and knit in garter stitch (i.e. every row knit) for 50 cm (20 in), then cast off. Fold the knitting in half and sew up the side seams. Make a strap by twisting four strands of yarn together and tie both ends of it to the bag.

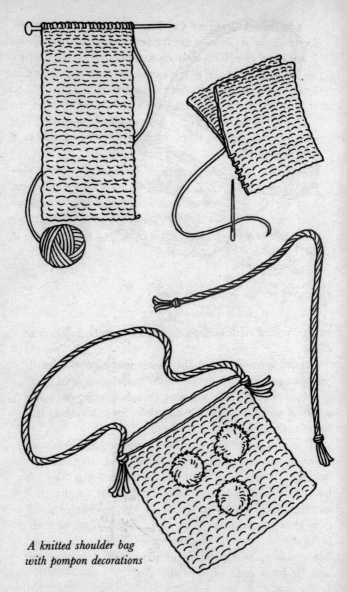

*A knitted shoulder bag
with pompon decorations*

You could decorate the bag with pompons on the front. Take a piece of cardboard about 10 cm wide by 7 cm deep (4 × 3 in) and wrap wool round it, starting by laying a piece across the top of the card with a longish loose end protruding. Wrap wool round the card until it looks fairly thick, then cut the wool and tie the cut end to the loose end you left in the beginning. Cut through the wound wool at the lower end of the card and you will have a pompon.

A dolly bag looks pretty if made from printed cotton. You will need about half a metre, depending on how large you want to make the bag. Make a paper pattern for the base first by drawing a circle 17.5 cm (7 in) in diameter on a sheet of paper and cutting it

Cutting out the base of the dolly bag

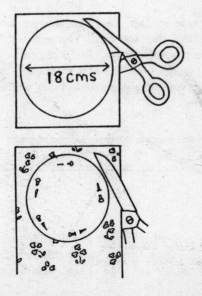

out. Pin this on one end of your material and cut it out. Then take a piece of fabric about 50 cm (20 in) long and 22 cm (8½ in) deep. Fold over the top centimetre (half inch) along one 50 cm side, folding the right

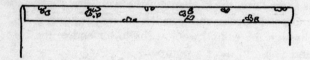

side over to the wrong side. Then fold over another 5 cm (2 in) and sew the edge down. It is best if you can

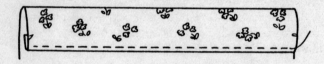

machine it, but if you cannot get hold of a sewing machine, then use small, neat stitches. When you have sewn the edge down, do another row of stitching 1.5 cm (¾ in) from the first to make a channel through which you can pass the drawstring which forms the bag's handle.

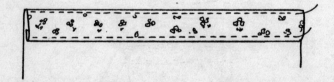

At the other 50 cm end of your material, sew with long, loose stitches a tacking thread about 1.5 cm (¾ in) from the cut edge. Then, with right sides together,

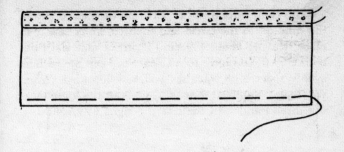

sew up the 22 cm sides of your material, about 1 cm (½ in) from the edge, starting the seam 1 cm below the hemmed top edge. (This is to allow you room to draw the cord through later.)

Pull the tacking thread to gather the fabric until you have a circular tube slightly smaller in diameter than the circle of fabric you cut out first.

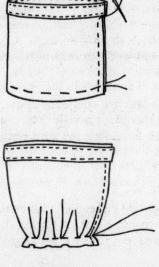

With right sides together, first pin the tacked end of the tube on to the circle and then carefully sew it in place, leaving about 1½ cm (¾ in) of material from both edges. You have to take care to keep the gathers evenly spaced, or your bag will look lopsided. When you have completed the seam, pull out the loose tacking thread and turn the bag the right way round.

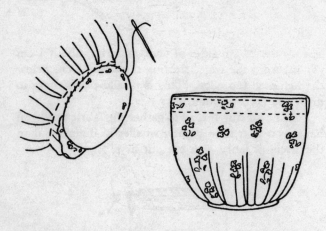

All that remains now is to pass a cord (a silky one, of the predominant colour of the bag, would look nice) through the channel left in the top of the bag. To help you do this fasten a safety pin to one end of the cord before you thread it through. You can push the safety pin through first, with the cord trailing behind, and manoeuvre the pin along from the outside quite easily. Be careful the other end of the cord doesn't go through the channel as well, or you will have to start again.

When you have threaded it through, tie both ends of the cord together and sew up the top part of the bag's seam, leaving the cord's tube ends open on the outside.

If you want your bag to have a firm base you can fit a piece of cardboard inside it after you have sewn it, with a layer of material stuck on the cardboard to form a lining to the bag.

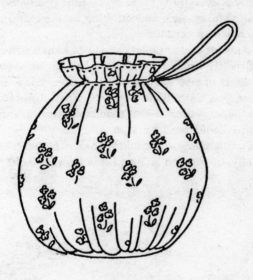

SPECS

If you have to wear specs try and get the most attractive pair you can find. This is not necessarily the most expensive pair, so spend some time looking around for the right frames. The top line of the frames should be roughly in line with your eyebrows. If it lies much above them you will have a foolish appearance; if it lies much below them you will tend to look rather miserable. Some opticians allow you to select frames of transparent plastic and have them dyed to whatever colour you choose, though once you have done this it is permanent, and you can't change your mind, so make sure you get it right in the first place.

It is important to get your specs just right, for you will look a lot better wearing them than peering short-sightedly at everything because you can't bear to be seen in your awful glasses, and suffering from eyestrain and headaches as a result.

If you want to jazz up an old pair of frames you could stick brightly coloured tape round them, or even use two colours of tape to give a striped effect. For a special occasion you could lightly coat the sides of the frames with a paper adhesive and sprinkle glitter on them — the same could be done with sunglasses.

For a silly party you could fix hair ornaments to the sides of your specs to give an Edna Everage look. Even

Jazzing up your specs

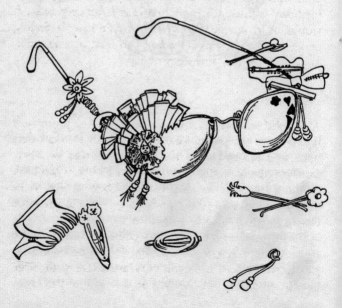

if you don't normally wear specs you could make enormous frames out of wire and decorate them with ornaments or flowers. Blu-tack would work very well to stick them on. You could make 'lenses' out of coloured cellophane paper for a really stunning look.

Try decorating sunglasses with tiny, colourful, stick-on paper cut-outs round the outer edges of the lenses, but remember not to let them cover up too much or you won't be able to see out of them.

JEWELLERY

When it comes to jewellery you can wear almost anything. At the time of writing there is a lot of big, bold 'ethnic' jewellery in the shops, and if you have a birthday coming up, or Christmas is getting near, it would be a wonderful present if someone is feeling generous. But quirky jewellery can look just as good, and be great fun and very cheap.

Necklaces

A piece of sequinned braid can make a very pretty and inexpensive choker necklace. You could sew on a tiny hook and eye to fasten it. Chokers can also be made from lengths of embroidered braid, which you can buy, or the Edwardian-looking velvet ribbon, which looks lovely with a pretty dress and can be made even more elegant with a brooch pinned to the front.

For a chunkier look, brightly coloured beads can be threaded on to lengths of thickish wool or on bootlaces. Leather bootlaces can look very attractive with large beads and can simply be tied at the back of the neck.

Put little spacer beads between the large ones and tie knots at each end of the row of beads to stop them falling off when you take the necklace off.

If you look at the button counter in a haberdasher's you may find delightful buttons in the shape of apples, mushrooms, teddy bears, and so on. Sewn on to a piece of ribbon these would make an unusual and charming necklace.

Delicate and beautiful silver necklaces are often made out of thin silver wire, with or without stones. You could make something similar for next to no cost out of 30-amp fuse wire (the sort used for cooker fuses), with glass beads, as in the illustration.

A necklace made from wire and glass beads

84

Bracelets

Lots of bracelets can be made in a similar way to the necklaces described above. Indeed, you could make a matching set. But instead of threading beads on to bootlaces or wire, for a bracelet thread them on to thin round elastic so you can just stretch it on and off your wrist.

In addition to bracelets, you can make wristlets out of knitted bands, or out of lace-trimmed fabric, to match your gloves. They look especially good with dainty fingerless gloves.

Brooches

The cheapest things to wear as brooches are badges. But if you get tired of a particular badge, why not stick tiny beads on it to make your own design for a brooch? You could make a bead guitar, or a country cottage, a lucky black cat or a butterfly, and you would end up with an original brooch that cost virtually nothing.

If you're keen on badges you can make your own out of cardboard with a safety pin taped to the back. To get an authentic-looking shiny finish, spray the badge with the kind of spray artists use, which works like a clear varnish. You can buy it in good stationers' and art shops.

Earrings

If your ears are pierced then you can buy a great range of earrings. But with a little ingenuity you can create amazing earrings of your own by using basic rings for pierced ears.

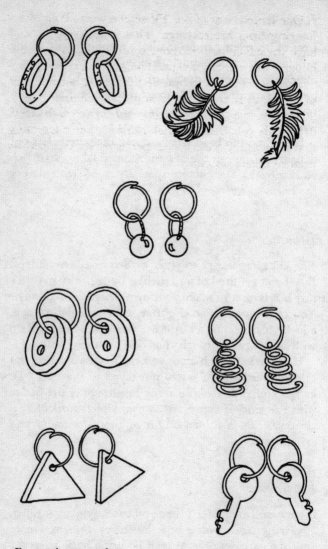

Fun earrings to make

One famous star of the TV screen wears Polo mints hanging from her earrings. They look terrific — and have the advantage that you can eat them if you get hungry! But you can hang all kinds of things from rings — charms off a charm bracelet, feathers, another pair of earrings (or one from each of two different pairs), little metal coils (the 30-amp fuse wire again) with pieces of brightly coloured material inside — almost anything that is light and looks either pretty or striking can be used to create an effect.

5. Craft techniques

A knowledge of how to perform crafts like sewing, embroidery, simple fabric printing and dyeing is a boon if you want to create individual and clever effects with clothes for very little financial outlay. Most people, however ham-fisted, can achieve a reasonably good effect if they take a little care and time over what they are doing, while others may discover they are very good at it. There is nothing very complicated in this chapter, just enough to give you a basic working knowledge of the individual techniques. If you find you enjoy them and are good at them, then you can go on to learn more.

SEWING

Of all the crafts that are useful to someone interested in clothes, sewing is the most important. On the next few pages you will find how to make individual stitches, including simple embroidery stitches, how to hem, how to bind a raw edge, how to sew on a pocket, and how to do simple appliqué and quilting.

One of the first points to consider when sewing is using the right type of thread and the right size needle for the job. Synthetic materials should be sewn with synthetic thread, cotton with cotton thread, silk with silk, and so on. If you are sewing a lightweight, flimsy material then you should use a very fine needle, whereas a heavy fabric such as tweed requires a much thicker, stronger needle. If you are interested in leather work you will have to buy a special needle, and seams on knitted woollen garments are best sewn up with wool threaded through a bodkin, or thick, blunt-ended needle.

When sewing one piece of fabric to another, pin or tack it in place first. This stops the pieces moving about and will in the end save you time.

If you are making a garment, or altering it, then be sure to press out any seams with an iron as you go along. Again, this may seem to take an unnecessary amount of time, but it will make all the difference to the finished look of the garment.

Hemming

Hemming is done to fasten off a raw edge to prevent it fraying. First of all about half a centimetre (a quarter of an inch) of the fabric is turned under from the right to the wrong side. Then another 2 cm (1 in) or so is turned under. It is often helpful to iron down the half-centimetre first, and then pin the next fold in place before starting to stitch.

Tie a knot in the end of the thread and run it through the folded-over fabric. Then put the needle through

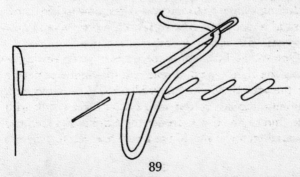

one thread only, if possible, of the main part of the fabric (the idea being not to let the stitch show on the right side) and take it through the fold of the hem edge. Repeat this procedure, working from right to left, until you have finished. To fasten off the thread make a number of small stitches in the folded-over part of the hem and finally run the thread through one to make a knot. Cut the thread, leaving just a short end.

Back stitch

This is a strong stitch which resembles machine stitching on the right side, but on the wrong side the stitches overlap. It is used to hand-sew seams. Insert the needle on the underside of the fabric and bring it through to the front. Then insert it to the right (i.e. behind) where the thread has come through and bring it up again in front of where the thread has come through. Push the needle back into the material adjacent to the left end of the first stitch you have made, and come up again one stitch's length in front. The stitches should be about 2 mm (one tenth of an inch) long and evenly spaced. Continue to the end of the seam then fasten off.

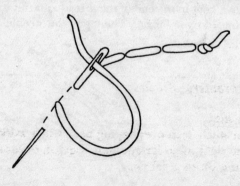

Running stitch

For a seam that does not need to be very strong, and for gathering, quilting and tacking, a running stitch is used. If intended as a permanent seam, it should consist of short, even stitches, but for gathering and tacking it can be longer, and use contrastingly coloured thread so it is easy to see. The needle is inserted into the wrong side of the material and pulled through to the right side, drawing the thread right through. It is then pushed through to the wrong side again and pulled back to the right side. The needle can be woven in and out so that several stitches can be sewn at once. The finished effect is of stitches and spaces of equal length. For a decorative effect, the spaces can be filled in with running stitches in a contrasting colour.

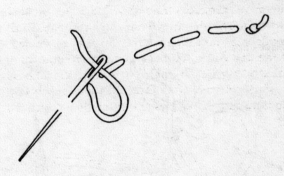

Embroidery stitches

Stem stitch
Stem stitch is an overlapping back stitch worked from left to right, used for outlining a motif, or for stitching writing on to a fabric.

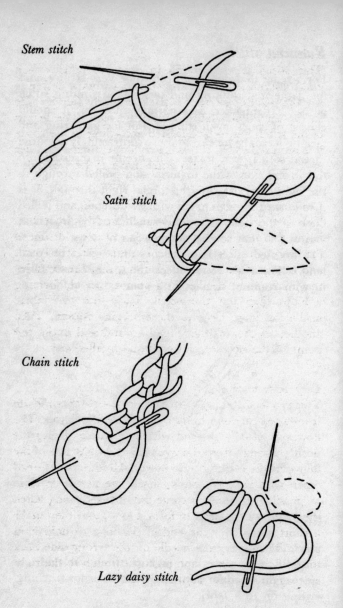

Stem stitch

Satin stitch

Chain stitch

Lazy daisy stitch

Satin stitch

This stitch is used to fill in areas of fabric when embroidering. Stitches are worked across a design — say the petal of a flower — packed tightly side by side so the underlying fabric cannot be seen. The length of the stitch has to be adjusted according to the space it is required to fill. If this is very large, then a number of smaller areas of satin stitch have to be worked.

Chain stitch

This is a decorative stitch worked from right to left. Bring the needle from the wrong to the right side of the fabric, then insert it again at almost the same point and take a stitch forwards, looping the thread under the point of the needle. Pull up the thread, forming a loop, then put the needle back into the fabric inside the loop, close to the emerging thread. Take another stitch with the thread around and under the point of the needle, and continue in this way.

Lazy daisy stitch

This is a form of chain stitch where the stitches radiate from a central point to form the petals of a flower. The flower is usually worked with five petals. Bring the needle through from the wrong to the right side of the fabric in the centre of the flower. Holding the thread down with your left hand, insert the needle as close as possible to where it came out. Make a long stitch the length of the petal to form a loop, and then make a short stitch over the end of the loop to hold it in place. Then carry the needle on the wrong side back to the flower's centre and push it through to the right side again to make another petal.

Binding a raw edge

If, for example, you have cut the sleeves of a shirt down to make a short-sleeved shirt, then you may want to bind the edge rather than hem it. It can be bound in a contrasting colour, or in the main body colour of a patterned fabric, to add interest.

With the edges of the tape and the fabric together, and the right side of the tape to the wrong side of the fabric, sew the tape on to the wrong side first. Then take it over the raw edge and fold the edge of the tape under before pinning it to the right side of the fabric. It should be so placed that it covers the stitches you have just made – i.e. there is more binding tape showing on the right side than on the wrong side. Hem it neatly in place, using tiny stitches underneath the fold of the tape, if possible, so they cannot be seen.

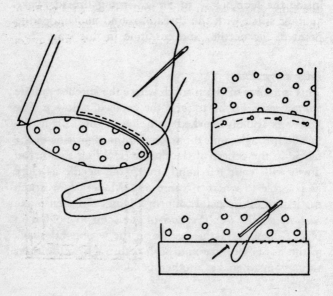

Sewing on a pocket

Pockets in contrasting colours can make a garment look a lot more fun — and have the added advantage of being useful. If, say, you have a red checked blouse or skirt, then add a bright red pocket. Or be even bolder and add a red pocket to a blue or green garment, or a bright green one to yellow or blue. On a striped garment add a pocket with the stripes going the opposite way. Look through the remnants counter of your local haberdasher's for scraps of brightly coloured material with which to make amusing pockets. They will cost you next to nothing and make your clothes completely individual and exciting.

For a shirt pocket you will need slightly less material than for a skirt or pair of trousers. Decide what size pocket you want and then add 1 cm (½ in) or so round the sides and bottom, and about 2-3 cm (1-1½ in) at the top to leave room for hemming. Fold under the 1 cm round the three sides, and at the top fold under

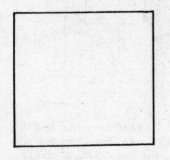
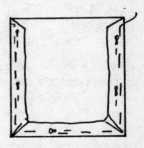

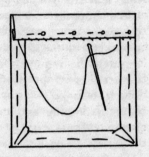

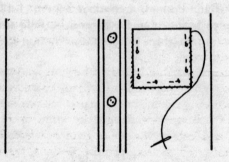

1 cm and then a further 2 cm. Pin and then sew this
in place, using a neat backstitch. Then pin and sew
the other three sides on to the garment – and there's
your pocket. You may like to sew matching breast
pockets on a shirt, or large, deep pockets on a skirt,
or even a small pocket on a sleeve. None will take you
very long to do.

BUTTONS

Buttons can transform a cardigan, jacket, shirt or dress. It is worth spending a bit of time hunting around, for really beautiful buttons can be found. Antiques stalls often sell exquisite buttons, though they can be expensive. A cheaper way of looking for interesting old buttons is to rummage through the clothes at jumble sales, for you may find an old dress or blouse for sale for 50p or so which has interesting buttons, even if you don't like the garment itself. If you are seeking old buttons it is worth looking through your mother's or grandmother's sewing drawer, as sometimes people keep the buttons long after the dress has gone.

There are many zany and attractive modern buttons, too. Go to a haberdasher's or large store and see what you can find. You will probably discover buttons in the form of hearts, stars, ladybirds, butterflies, apples and other fruits, bows, teddy bears, sweets — and many other interesting things.

In general, brightly coloured buttons featuring toys and so on look good on plain brightly coloured clothes of a contrasting colour; pretty, pastel buttons look good on more delicate lacy designs in white or in pastel colours; and leather, wooden or leather-covered buttons are suitable on heavy, chunky designs for rugged outdoor wear. Children used to have silver buttons on their best party frocks, but these would be very expensive nowadays. You can, however, buy cheap metal buttons which resemble silver, gold or bronze and which can look very pretty. You can also buy button shapes which are meant to be covered with fabric but which you could have fun painting with amusing faces or whatever.

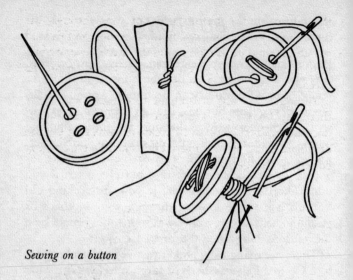

Sewing on a button

To sew on a button, thread a suitably-sized needle with either single or double thread, depending on the size of the button. Tie a knot in one end and secure the thread with a couple of small stitches on the wrong side of the fabric before pushing it through to the button on the right side. For a four-hole button, first take the needle and thread through two buttonholes diagonally opposite each other for four stitches; next bring the thread up through the material to the other holes and repeat the stitches across the other diagonal. Then bring the needle through to the right side of the material underneath the button and wind the thread round the threads securing the button two or three times. Take the needle back to the wrong side and fasten off the thread with two or three small stitches.

If you are sewing a button on to thick material you will need to leave a 'shank' of thread between the button and the fabric of approximately the same thickness as the fabric, or the button will not pass through the buttonhole. When you have finished sewing on this kind of button, wind the thread round the shank several times until it is completely covered before fastening off the thread.

Although buttons are meant to be sewn on where there are butonholes, you can just sew them on for decoration. You could even create an amusing picture or slogan using plain coloured buttons in a contrasting colour to the garment.

A button 'flower'

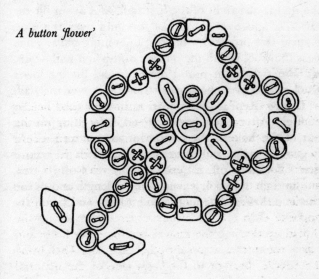

FRENCH KNITTING

This is a very easy way of producing narrow tubes of 'knitting' which can be used for headbands, belts, the paws of the cat scarf (see page 65), or can be sewn on to sweaters in interesting shapes to make appliqué motifs. You need a cotton reel (preferably an old wooden one though a plastic one will do), four thin nails or pins, a crochet hook and some wool.

Ask an adult to hammer the four nails or pins into one end of the cotton reel (on a plastic one, hammer them into the four struts round the central hole), evenly spaced and about 3 mm ($^{1}/_{10}$ in) from the hole. Wind the wool twice round the first nail, then with the crochet hook lift the lower strand of wool over the upper strand and over the top of the nail. Wind the wool twice round the nail to the right of the first nail, and again lift the lower strand over the upper one and over the nail. Repeat this process on the two remaining nails. Then pass the wool round the outside of the first nail again, without twisting it round the nail, and lift the lower wool strand over the upper strand and over the nail, as before. Repeat this process until your tube is long enough. After a few rounds you will see it appearing out of the hole in the bottom of the cotton reel. As it grows longer, pull it gently downwards to keep it firm. To fasten off, lift each loop of wool off its nail, cut through the wool, leaving a 15 cm length and thread this end through the loops. Pull it tight and tie off the end.

APPLIQUÉ

Appliqué is a French word meaning applied, and we use it to mean a decorative motif cut from one material and glued or sewn on ('applied') to another. Felt is a good material to use if the garment to which it is applied is not going to be washed, as it does not fray. But cotton or other material can be used, cut slightly larger than required and hemmed round the edge with the cut edge tucked in. In general you should use a fabric of the same weight or lighter than that of the garment.

You may like to design your own motif or copy something out of a book or magazine. But keep it simple. Experiment with paper shapes first — perhaps cutting out a paper circle, folding it in four and then cutting bits out of it. When you decide on your design, make a template out of paper and use it to cut out your fabric. Remember if it is a fabric which will fray to cut out 1 cm (½ in) or so extra all the way round to allow for hemming. If the motif is to be placed

Cutting out and pinning on an appliqué motif

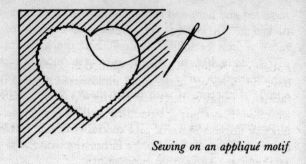

Sewing on an appliqué motif

centrally, say on a pocket, then fold the garment first vertically and then diagonally, and where the folds cross position the centre of the motif. Pin it on to the garment, and then sew it, either using small, almost invisible stitches, or using a bold stitch in a contrasting colour to make it part of the design.

If you don't want to sew it on you can buy special bonding material with a paper backing, which should be cut to a shape slightly larger than the motif and then ironed to the wrong side of the motif material. Allow it to cool and then trim the edges to the shape of the motif. Peel off the backing cloth, place the motif right side up on the garment and iron it in place, using a steam iron or a dry iron with a damp cloth.

You can even stick motifs in place using a fabric adhesive. But this may well come unstuck when the garment is washed.

To make a more complicated motif you may wish to add one feature on top of another, or to embroider fine detail in place. But don't try and make your design too complicated or it may look over-fussy, and you may resent ever having started it. And don't forget that you can use appliqué for a practical purpose – such as the decorative patching of a hole.

QUILTING

Fabric can be bought already quilted and used to make bags or clothing, or you can make your own quilted fabric. It requires three layers: the top layer of fabric, which will be seen; the padding, which can be an old piece of thickish material or a special synthetic padding; and the lining, which can be either the same material as the outer layer or a plain fabric.

Quilting can be used to make attractive bags, such as that described on pages 77– 81 in Chapter 4, for waistcoats, jackets, and so on. It looks pretty and gives warmth without a great deal of weight.

If you are going to create your own quilting, tack the three layers of material together first. When doing the actual stitching it is best to use straight parallel lines, squares or diamond shapes – curves are much more difficult to do. Work a grid across your fabric from side to side and top to bottom. If you are using a sewing machine you may need to adjust the thread tension and reduce the pressure on the presser foot so the fabric passes under without the fullness being pushed in front of it. You can buy special quilting attachments for machines if you intend doing a lot of quilting.

You may wish to quilt just part of a fabric rather than all of it in geometric patterns. For example, if you have a fabric with a bold design, such as a large flower, you could quilt just round the flower or flowers. Tack the three layers of fabric together first to prevent them slipping (see **1**). Then stitch round the design, starting from the innermost part of it (for example, if it is a flower, start in the centre) and working outwards, stitching along the edge of each shape (see **2**). Finish off the sewing by taking the thread through to the wrong

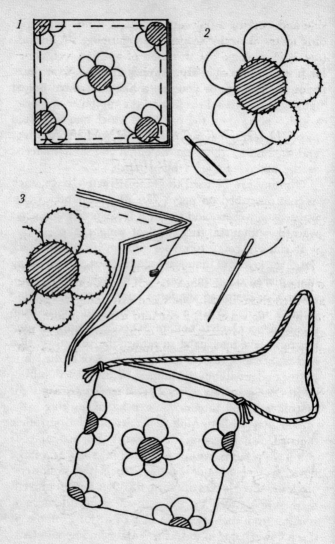

Quilted flowers on a bag

side and working a few centimetres of it into the padding material until it is 'lost', then snipping off the end (see 3). You could use this kind of quilting technique for just one side of a bag, leaving the rest plain, but if you do this you will need to line the whole bag.

SIMPLE FABRIC-PRINTING TECHNIQUES

Fabric printing is an easy way of creating a unique design as well as being great fun to do. You can use it to print a design just on a pocket or shirt front, or all over a fabric.

The easiest way to make a printing block is to use a potato. The potato should be scrubbed thoroughly first and then sliced in half, the sliced side being the printing area. This has to be cut into a shape before you can use it for printing, for it is the raised surface left after cutting that does the printing. Or you can cut

Some shapes that can be cut from a potato to make printing blocks

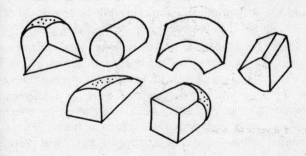

the potato-half into a three-dimensional geometric shape, such as a pyramid, cylinder or cube, to give you a block with a number of possible printing surfaces.

For your colours use cold-water dyes. If they come in powder form mix them with water according to the manufacturer's instructions, then apply them to the potatoes with a paintbrush. Take care not to splash them around, and wear rubber gloves to avoid getting them on your hands. Press the potato down gently but firmly on to the fabric. If you are going to repeat the pattern, paint more dye on to the potato each time if you want to have an evenly-coloured result. If, however, you want to have some gradual fading of colour, then keep using the potato without any more dye on it. If you are using more than one colour use different potatoes for each, and if your printing is spread over more than one day then cut new blocks each day, for the potatoes are likely to go rubbery. The cold-water dyes should give a colour-fast result, but follow the instructions carefully and wash the fabric carefully afterwards or your design may be ruined.

Some ideas for prints using blocks cut from potatoes are on pages 107 and 108. When working on a complicated design, such as the bunch of grapes, draw it first with a thick black outline on paper and place it under the fabric so you can see the pattern through the fabric and use it as a guide for placing the blocks. If using two colours, then let one dry before applying the other.

Other vegetables and fruits make good printing blocks, too. Onions, for example, can be cut in half horizontally to give a beautiful pattern of layered rings, but if you cut one vertically you will get quite a different pattern. The central cores of carrots can be removed to form rings; celery sticks cut across make pretty, crinkled half-moon shapes; and apples, pears and green

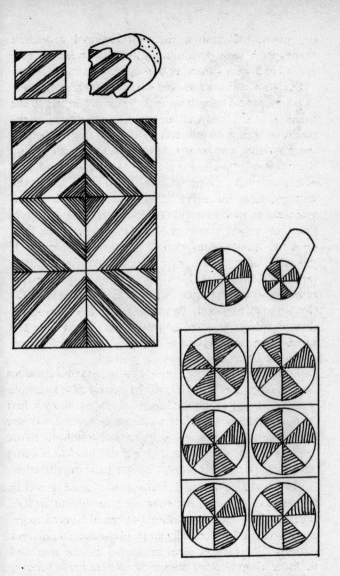

Some shapes and designs that can be created from potato blocks

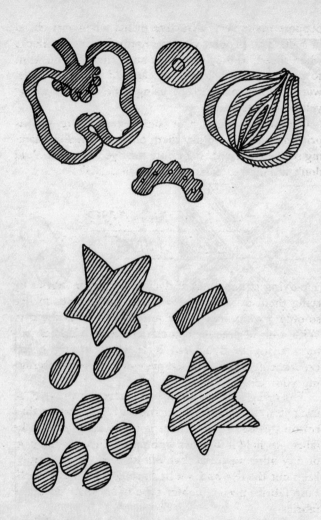

Peppers, carrots, onions and celery make good printing blocks.

A bunch of grapes can be created using blocks to print the leaves and stalk and fingertips to print the grapes.

peppers make very attractive prints when just sliced in half. The peppers become natural printing blocks when sliced, as they have only an outline. If you want to print a pepper shape you can add the seeds afterwards with a paintbrush, using little dabs of white, yellow or red paint.

Choose only firm fruit and vegetables to use as printing blocks, and dry them on a cloth before starting so their juice doesn't dilute the dye too much. And don't attempt to eat them afterwards!

TIE-DYEING AND BLEACHING

Tie-dying is a method of dyeing clothes or fabrics by tying them in clumps before immersing them in dye so only certain areas come into contact with the dye. With a bit of practice you can create all kinds of patterns using tie-dying, so it is worth trying a few experiments first with an old piece of cloth before sacrificing your new T-shirt.

The tying medium must be resistant to the dye, so use nylon thread or cord, or rubber bands, rather than cotton thread or string. But you can simply knot the fabric, or hold it together with paper clips, clothes pegs or any other material that will hold the fabric firmly, keep out the dye and not be harmed by the dye itself. Fine fabrics need a lighter type of tie than do heavy fabrics.

You will need an old saucepan, an enamelled bucket or some other kind of utensil for use as a dye bath. If this means borrowing something from the kitchen then do check with your mum first that it is OK to

Tie-dyeing techniques and their effects:

A simple knot

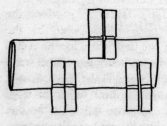

Clothes pegs

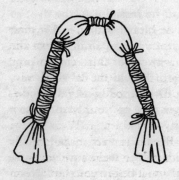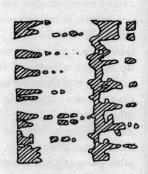

Binding with thread

do so, as the dye bath is going to be a bit messy for kitchen use afterwards.

Natural fibres are the easiest fabrics to tie-dye, as they are receptive to dye and will absorb cold-water dyes. Synthetic fibres often need a hot-water dye, which makes them difficult to wash afterwards without the colour running, and fabrics with special finishes cannot be dyed. If you are a beginner, therefore, stick to cotton fabrics to start with. The cloth should be clean and uncreased before you start.

When using dyes, take great care not to splash them around and wear rubber gloves to protect your hands.

Having tied or knotted the fabric to produce the desired pattern, mix the dye as instructed by the manufacturer and immerse the tied fabric for the stated time. Then take it out, rinse it thoroughly, and leave it tied up until you are sure it is dry all the way through. This may take some time with a thick fabric or large garment, but if you untie it before it is dry the dye will seep into the uncoloured areas and ruin the pattern. When you are sure it is safe to untie the ties, do it very carefully, and if you have to cut them take great care not to cut the fabric as well.

Certain fabrics can be tie-bleached to give a reverse effect. This is suitable for cottons, especially jeans and fabrics that are not absolutely colour-fast. You will end up with a white and coloured design. Be very, very careful when using bleach. Do not spill it on your clothes or skin, and if you do get any on your skin wash it off immediately with plenty of cold water. Wear rubber gloves as a protection. Bleach is such a potentially dangerous product that it is best to make sure you have your parents' permission to use it before you start. Never let small children anywhere near it — it is poisonous when drunk. Dilute the bleach according to the manufacturer's instructions for bleaching clothes.

If you are ambitious and just a little bit brave you can get some superb effects from tie-dyeing. You could try using two colours, having two dyebaths ready simultaneously. Put the tied cloth into the first dyebath, then make more ties and put it into a second colour. The dyes will blend, so that eventually your first ties will end up with a white pattern (assuming your cloth was white to start with), your second ties will have the colour of the first dyebath (let's say it was red), and the cloth which was exposed throughout will be a blend of the first and second dyebath colours. So if the second dyebath was blue your cloth will end up purple, with red and white designs on it. Don't forget to rinse the fabric thoroughly between each dyeing, and only untie the ties when you are sure it is completely dry.

6. Skin deep

Our skin is the largest organ in our bodies, covering an area of roughly 1.7 square metres (2 square yards). It is supplied with lots of tiny nerve endings which register feelings of touch, heat, cold and pain. And it performs the vital function of keeping our body temperature constant. When we are cold, tiny muscles in the skin act to reduce its surface area, producing the familiar 'goose pimples', and decreasing the area from which heat can be lost. When we are hot, the veins near the surface of the skin dilate, to help them lose heat, and sweat glands in the skin cover its surface with water. As this water evaporates it uses heat from our bodies to do so, which takes heat from our bodies and helps keep us cool.

To keep it supple and waterproof, skin is supplied with glands called sebaceous glands, which produce an oily substance called sebum. Some people have more sebaceous glands than others – generally dark people have more than fair people – which is why some skins are dry and flaky and some are greasy. It is the blocking and subsequent infection of these tiny glands that cause spots and pimples, and it is because the glands are particularly active in our teens, due to hormonal changes in our bodies, that the dreaded acne occurs. Our environment also has an effect on whether our skins are dry or greasy. Central heating, or too much exposure to sunlight, or very cold, windy weather, all tend to make the skin dry.

The pigment, or colouring, of the skin is called melanin, and it is the amount of melanin we have that determines whether we have light- or dark-coloured skins. People from the hot, sunny countries of the world have a lot of melanin in their skins to protect them from the sun's rays, whereas people from cooler, less sunny climates have less. However, what melanin they do have is activated by exposure to sunlight, which is why normally white skin goes brown in the sun.

These days it is fashionable for white people to sport suntans, but the fashion has only been around for the last sixty years or so. Before that people went to great lengths to preserve the whiteness of their skins, believing that a suntanned appearance would make them resemble labourers who worked out of doors, instead of ladies and gentlemen of the leisured classes. As was mentioned in Chapter 1, the suntan fashion was 'invented' in the 1920s on the French Riviera by the dress designer Gabrielle 'Coco' Chanel. She and her followers were called by the newspaper gossips of the time *'les petites chocolatières'* – the little chocolate drops – but the idea caught on, and since then the tanned look has been the thing to have. Nowadays it is supposed to show that people have the leisure and wealth to lie around in the sun, often in exotic parts of the world, instead of working in an office all day.

Some people carry the tanning idea to extremes and end up with skins like old leather, or, as the medical experts remind us nowadays, with skin cancer. But if tanning is done slowly, carefully and in moderation, it is good for the skin and for the body generally. It clears up blemishes like acne, stimulates the growth of the skin's cells, produces vitamin D in the body, which helps it to absorb calcium, and gives a general feeling of well-being. If you want to get a suntan, you should never stay in the sun long enough to burn your skin. Start off by exposing it for only about half an hour on the first day, then increase the time by half an hour a day to give your skin time to adjust. Fair-skinned people need to take more care about this than do dark-skinned people, and if you are in a hot country half an hour may be too long at first. Avoid the midday sun to start with, and apply a protective tanning lotion or cream at frequent intervals. These are often graded for different kinds of skin so you should be able to find one that suits you. After you have washed or had a bath, it is a good idea to rub a moisturizing lotion into your skin if it tends to be on the dry side, to keep it supple.

Your skin reflects your general health, and it is no use expecting it to look good if you live on fizzy drinks, pastries and chips, and don't get a reasonable amount of fresh air and exercise. Lack of sleep, too, often affects your skin badly. So if you want your skin to look good, try and get regular exercise, lots of fresh air, plenty of sleep, and eat a sensible diet. This means eating foods called proteins (which are contained in meat, fish, eggs, cheese, milk, nuts and certain grain products), and vitamin-rich fruits, salads and vegetables, along with cereals and wholemeal bread to give further vitamins, minerals and roughage. Drink fruit juices and ordinary water in preference to lots of cups of tea and coffee and fizzy drinks. No amount of make-up or lotions can put vitality into the skin of someone who is unhealthy and tired.

CLEANSING

Up to now this chapter has been concerned with skin care in general, but from here on it is concerned with faces. We all know that we should wash our bodies once a day to keep them sweet-smelling and healthy – but should we wash our faces? There are lots of theories about the best way to clean your face. Some people say you should never use soap and water on it, but should use special cleansing lotions formulated to suit your particular skin type. This can mean using two different lotions if your skin is greasy down the central area (forehead, nose and chin) and drier at the sides. Other people swear by soap and water. It is largely a matter of personal preference, though there are times when washing with soap and water can make the skin feel a lot more refreshed than cleaning it with a lotion and cotton wool.

Whatever way you decide to cleanse your face, tailor the routine (and the products used, whether they be lotions or soaps) to your skin type. If your skin is greasy you can treat it a little more roughly than if it is dry, but whatever your skin type, you should cleanse it twice a day. If you do use soap on a dry skin make sure it is a very mild soap, such as a baby soap, and rinse it off thoroughly. In general highly perfumed soaps are not suited to dry skins. Specially sensitive skins can be treated with preparations made specially for them.

Even if you prefer washing your face to using lotions on it, you will probably have to use special cosmetics like eye make-up remover if you wear eye make-up, as mascara doesn't come off very well with soap and water and makes an awful mess of the face cloth.

After cleansing, the use of an astringent lotion will

close the pores of a greasy skin, and the application of a moisturizing lotion will help to keep a dry skin from flaking. If the skin of your face is half and half, then use the astringent on the greasy panel and the moisturizer on the rest.

MAKE-UP

Whether or not you wear make-up is for you and your parents to decide, but most people probably agree with a general rule that it is not suitable to wear for school but is OK for a special evening out. When you get older you may still agree with that rule, and not wear make-up in the daytime, or you may decide to wear it all the time, but even then most people think that a little make-up looks a lot better than a heavily plastered face. Apart from when we are trying to create a special effect, say for a party, most of us try and look 'naturally beautiful', rather than artificially made up. It wasn't always the case. The ladies of ancient Greece and Rome used to use a white lead substance to whiten their skins, not realizing it was poisonous, and in Edwardian times ladies used to sponge a liquid white substance (rather like shoe whitener) on their faces, necks, shoulders and arms. Like shoe whitener this product tended to crack and go powdery as it dried, which meant that their faces literally cracked on the surface if they held an animated conversation, and traces of whitener would be found all over their clothes. To give a delicate blush to their cheeks and an inviting redness to their lips they used to nip the skin between finger and thumb, or, in the case of their lips, between their teeth, for only ladies of ill repute wore cosmetics to colour their faces. It wasn't until the 1930s that make-up came to be considered respectable for decent women to wear.

Now that most women consider make-up to be an acceptable part of life, let's look at the basic rules and effects, with some especially exciting ideas for parties included as we go along.

First of all make sure you have all the necessary equipment as well as the actual make-up. You will need cotton wool, paper tissues, a hairband or clips to hold your hair out of the way, and make-up brushes.

Cleanse your skin thoroughly before you start, and apply moisturizer or astringent if you use it. The first part of make-up to put on is foundation, an all-over covering cream, mousse, gel or liquid which will hide any blemishes and can make the skin look paler or tanned, if that is what you want. Or it can just give you a nice, healthy glow. Some foundations give a shinier finish than others, so make sure you choose one that suits both your skin and the effect you want to create. You may not want to use foundation at all, feeling that it will produce too 'made-up' an effect, but it is useful if you are putting on make-up for a special occasion.

Instead of foundation you may like to use an all-in-one formula that includes both foundation and powder. This has the advantage that you can put it on very thinly or more thickly for a more matt effect, and it is useful for those partially greasy skins, as you can apply a thicker coat over the greasy areas. Girls always used to be told to apply powder over foundation to 'set' it, but this can produce a heavy, middle-aged look and is best kept for special times when you are going in for an almost theatrical effect. Powder is sometimes useful dusted lightly over the skin without foundation underneath if you just want a very light covering to mask blemishes or a greasy skin. You can dab it on with a powder puff, with cotton wool, or even with a tissue, but it is best applied with a special make-up brush, which will whisk it lightly over your face, rather than leaving dabs of it here and there.

blusher

Blushers are usually applied with a brush, too, though with a smaller one than is used for powder. They are used to shape your face, and to highlight your cheekbones, as well as to give a warm, healthy glow. They come in a range of colours, from pink to brownish-red. You can buy little palettes of blushers with different colours in them, which are fun to try out, but if you are buying them singly try and choose one to suit your skin colour as well as the general effect you are trying to create. In general, girls with pale skins and fair hair should choose the pinker tones, while girls with darker skins should choose the reds and earthy colours. The usual place to apply blusher is to the cheeks, but if you're feeling adventurous you can also brush a little between your eyebrows and on your chin to give you a warm glow. For specially glamorous occasions, you can buy blushers with a gold tinge to them. They would look particularly good on a tanned skin.

Along with blushers go highlighters. In the face-shaping business, blushers create the hollows and highlighters emphasize the bone structure. They are applied to the cheekbones, the forehead bones and along the bony arch just below the eyebrow. Highlighters come in all kinds of gold, silver and pearlized effects — which can be great fun for parties. But if you haven't got and can't afford to buy any you can cheat by applying lightly a fairly greasy cream — Vaseline, for example — which will shine when it catches the light in just the same way.

highlights

Eye Make-Up

Of all the different kinds of make-up eye make-up is the most fun. There is a huge range of colours and products to choose from, and you can create the most amazing effects, from just lightly emphasizing your natural features to creating huge and dramatic Cleopatra-type eyes for a party.

You will need soft eye pencils, eye shadow and mascara. Outline your eyes close to the lashes with a soft, smudgy pencil. This can either be a brownish or greyish colour, to tone with your eyelashes, or a more adventurous colour such as blue, green, red or lilac to tone with your eye shadow. Avoid black unless you have really dark eyes and hair, or unless you want to look like a punk. You may like to use the pencil to outline the eye socket area, too, or this can be done with a darker shade of eye shadow.

Your choice of colour for eye shadow depends on the colour of your eyes, the colour of your clothes, and how adventurous you are feeling. For an everyday, non-startling effect, a little neutral-toned shadow, such as one of the greyish or brownish colours, is fine. But if you want to be more dramatic choose a colour such as blue, green, lilac or even red or yellow to tone with your clothes. (Yellow eyeshadow applied all the way round your eyes will really stop people in their tracks!)

It is also fun to use two or more different shades of eye shadow at the same time, though make sure both eyes match! For bluish coloured clothes, use a pink-lilac shadow on the inner part of the lids and a blue-grey one on the outer part, blending them subtly together where they overlap in the middle. For warmer toned clothes, such as yellow, orange or red, try using a yellow shadow on the inner part of the eyelids and red on the outer. For green clothes use yellow on the inner area and green on the outer; for turquoise or jade-coloured clothes, use green on the inner area and blue on the outer. If you are wearing white you can

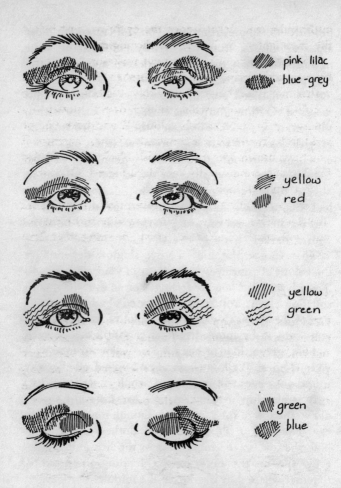

pink lilac
blue-grey

yellow
red

yellow
green

green
blue

wear whatever colours you like. The blue-green colours will give a cool effect and would go with a pinkish lipstick, the red-yellow-orange-brown colours would give a brighter effect and should be toned with a redder lipstick and matching blusher. You can, of course, with any of the above suggestions, use a third colour to outline the eye socket under the eyebrow, just below the highlighter, or instead of the highlighter.

The finishing touch to your eye make-up is provided by mascara. Again, there are a number of colours from which to choose, but for every day it is best to choose a colour that emphasizes, though doesn't drastically change, your natural lash colour. If you have fair or reddish hair, then use a brownish or grey mascara; if you have brown hair use brownish-black; and only use black if you are naturally very dark-haired. Of course, if you want to look like a punk . . .

For special effects you can buy mascara in colours like dark blue and green, but you have to be careful how you use them or the effect can be silly rather than freaky.

Party Eyes

Gold and silver come into their own here, with all the colours of the rainbow. Try using gold eyeshadow on the under-brow area, shading to green on the inner part of the eyelid and brown on the outer part, adding a touch of gold below the eye. Or use silver on the underbrow area and below the eye, blue on the inner

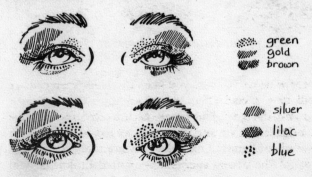

green
gold
brown

silver
lilac
blue

eyelids and lilac on the outer lids. Shade the gold or silver outwards from the outer corners of the eyes and add a few gold or silver 'freckles' over your cheek bones. 'Freckles' are fun and can be added in other colours, too, over your cheekbones and the bridge of your nose to match a spotted fabric. Dip a small paintbrush into cream eyeshadow and just dot them on. But take care where and when you do this – you don't want to be accused of having measles!

A scattering of freckles can make an attractive effect

Most people don't need to use eyebrow pencils, though if you are very fair you may like to darken your eyebrows slightly. Otherwise they are probably best left alone. Pluck them enough to tidy up the shape but not to change it drastically or it can give you a foolish appearance. But for a party you can achieve a wild look by brushing your eyebrow hairs upwards, and adding a few extra 'hairs' with an eye pencil. Or you could brush them smooth and put a little Vaseline on them to give them a sleek and glossy wet look. If you are going in for the gold and silver look you could enhance it with a little glitter on the eyebrows.

If you want to make Cleopatra eyes for a special party then you can go to town with the black eyeliner, mascara and eyebrow pencil. Outline the eyes in heavy black and carry the line outwards and upwards, to meet a line coming down from the eyebrows. Fill in the area between the eyeliner and the eyebrows with different-coloured eyeshadows, as described above, carrying a little eyeshadow under the eye beneath the eyeliner. Finish with several layers of mascara, allowing each to dry before applying the next. If the lashes become too stuck together, separate them by brushing with a clean mascara-brush.

Lips

Magazines often advise using a lip brush to apply lipstick, but it is not necessary unless you fancy yourself as a model. Applying lipstick takes a bit of practice. Try and follow your natural lip outline. If you try and accentuate it too much beyond the natural you will look rather silly — a bit like the early silent film beauties look to us now with their 'cupid's bows'. Again, lipsticks come in a multitude of colours and choosing one that looks right can be difficult. It is all very well trying the colour out on the inside of your wrist in the time-honoured fashion, but that will not really show you what the colour will look like on your lips, for it doesn't take your natural lip colour into account. Bright red lips will look reddish through a pale pink lipstick, bluish-toned lips will turn some pinks to mauve, and so on. If you can't get the colour you want, then try wearing one colour over another. A yellow lipstick worn under a pink one will make the pink more orange. You can achieve an interesting effect by outlining your lips in a slightly darker colour than your main colour, or by outlining them in yellow and then using a pink lipstick. Lip gloss can be used over lipstick to give a shiny effect, or on its own for a natural, glossy look. Some lip glosses are lightly coloured and these too can be used either alone or over an existing colour to achieve an effect. If you have two or three differently-toned lipsticks you can have great fun mixing the colours together to see what effects you can produce.

If your lips get very dry, then use lip-salve either under your lipstick or just on its own. It will provide a slightly glossy look and protect your lips from the drying effects of the sun and from cold winter winds.

If you like the idea of using cosmetics but are put off by what you may have read about products being tested on animals, then contact Beauty Without Cruelty Ltd, 37 Avebury Avenue, Tonbridge, Kent TN9 1TL, who will tell you about cosmetics which are produced without animal products or animal testing.

7. Crowning glory

'Hair,' so the saying goes, 'is woman's crowning glory'. And so it was, in the days when it was worn as long as it would grow and elaborately curled and twisted into hairstyles that were miracles of engineering. The dressing of her hair must have taken up a good deal of a woman's time in the early part of this century, though of course most of the people who wore really elaborate styles had personal maids to help them.

Today we are lucky because we can wear our hair in any style we like, from long and elaborately curled styles to those so short they can scarcely be brushed. But whatever style you choose to wear your hair in it is important to keep it healthy. Your hair, like your skin, reflects your general health and diet – you may have noticed how dull and lifeless it becomes when you've been in bed with flu or had a heavy cold.

People have between 90,000 and 150,000 individual hairs on their heads, with blondes having the greatest number and redheads the lowest. Each hair grows about 1 cm (½ in) a month from its individual follicle (or root), and it is the shape of the follicle that determines whether the hair is straight or curly. Each follicle has a sebaceous gland which secretes sebum to keep the hair and scalp supple and in good condition. It is the degree of activity of the sebaceous glands that determines whether you have dry or greasy hair. Every day people lose about 100 of their hairs, which are replaced by new hairs growing, though the replacement rate can slow down in times of illness. When the hair is wet it is porous and swells slightly, which is why people curl or straighten their hair when it is wet rather than when it is dry.

Hair should always be kept clean, for whatever style you choose will be spoilt if it is dirty. Daily brushing helps to remove loose hairs and dust, and is beneficial to dry hair as it stimulates the sebaceous glands and helps to distribute the oil along the hair. But it can be disastrous for greasy hair, as it makes it even more greasy. If your hair is greasy it may need washing every day, or every other day, but you may be able to leave dry hair for a week without washing it. You shouldn't leave it longer, though.

Choose a shampoo that suits your kind of hair. If you do have to wash your hair every day or two it is best to avoid the 'for greasy hair' shampoos as they tend to dry out the scalp, which then over-reacts by producing still more grease. When you wash your hair, unless it is very dirty, use just one lot of shampoo. Wet the hair thoroughly all over, squeeze the shampoo into your hands and then spread it evenly all over the hair, using circular movements with your fingertips to work it right down to the roots. Rinse thoroughly with lots of water. After rinsing the hair should squeak when rubbed between finger and thumb, and if it does it proves it is clean. If it isn't, you may need to apply another lot of shampoo, but be sure to rinse thoroughly again or your hair will not look clean and shiny. If you use a conditioner, apply it after rinsing, comb it through gently, leave it for a minute, and then rinse it off. With greasy hair it is as well not to condition right down to the roots but just to do the ends. Squeeze the water out of your hair and then wrap a towel round it, squeezing it gently to take out the excess water.

Dry hair can be improved by rubbing warmed olive oil into the scalp before washing. It should be covered with a towel and left for as long as possible before washing it off. Greasy hair can be improved by a final rinse to which a dessertspoonful of lemon juice has been added (for fair hair) or vinegar (for dark hair).

Having got your hair clean you may just want to comb it through and let it dry naturally, or you may want to style it. This can be done by blow drying – winding the hair round a brush and drying it with a hand-held dryer to give it lift and bounce; using rollers, either ordinary ones on wet hair which is dried with them in place or heated ones which are used on dry hair; plaiting to give waves to long, straight hair; or rough blow drying with the hair allowed to fall upside down so it doesn't lie too flat on the head when it is dry. You can also use heated brushes and curling tongs on dry hair to produce curls, ringlets or just curves.

There are various styling aids to help you. Mousse is really a kind of setting lotion that helps to keep the hair in the shape you want it. Some types give a stronger 'hold' than others so choose one that is right for you. They can be used on dry hair too, but tend to make it feel sticky. Gels are stronger versions of mousse which allow you to make your hair into almost any shape. Glazes are similar, but come in liquid form. Applied to wet hair they help to give it extra volume and to hold it in place; applied to dry hair they give it rigidity, so if you're after a punk hairdo then they're what you need. If you use any of the above styling aids, be sure to wash them out thoroughly afterwards.

After styling, comb your hair lightly into place. To keep it there you may want to use a hair spray. These

too come in different strengths and it is advisable to use
the lightest one you can, or you may get the rigid 'set'
look that middle-aged women go round with. Close your
eyes when using hair spray and try not to breathe in
at the time of actually spraying. Again, hair spray
should be thoroughly washed out of the hair at the next
hair-washing session.

Here are some freaky hairstyles to try.

If your hair is straight and bobbed, try this style using
wet-look gel. Shape the front part or fringe into a large
curl with strong-hold gel, then hold it in place with
a strong-hold hair spray.

The same length hair can be twisted into a pony tail
on top of the head, then twisted back through the pony
tail loop to form a small knot. The loose ends are then
gelled into spikes, as is the fringe.

The same length or longer hair can be made to look like this. It is fluffed out with strong-hold mousse into shape and then sprayed with strong-hold hair spray.

Short hair can be moussed into shape, and either all brought forwards or parted at the side.

Or it can be blown dry into this sophisticated shape and sprayed to hold it in place.

If hair is of varying lengths it can be gelled into a semi-punk spiky effect.

This haircut is very neat and takes no looking after at all — just a bit of gel to spike up the front hair.

Strong gel can be used to transform a neat bob into this amazing look for parties.

If your hair is layered you can achieve this windswept
look by waxing the ends.

Finally, for a special party only – what about this? It's a pity we can't show it in colour, for those brush-shaped ends are meant to be sprayed with rainbow colours! You would need help to achieve this style, for it is difficult to work on top of your head. It is produced by glazing the hair, dividing it into small sections, and then fanning out the sections' ends. After that, spray-on colour can be used to create the rainbow effect.

COLOURING YOUR HAIR

There are a number of different ways of colouring your hair, and the more permanent they are the more they should be approached with caution. It may sound awfully fuddy-duddy, but your natural hair colour is likely to be the one that suits you, and while it is fun to spray on a special colour for a party it is quite another thing to have to live with it for months while it grows out.

Rinses, coloured mousses and spray- or brush-on colours are all temporary devices that can be washed out with one shampoo. They show to the best advantage on blonde hair, and are quite safe to experiment with, as you can simply wash them out if you don't like the result. So if you want to have pink curls for a party, go ahead!

Then there are semi-permanent colours which last for up to twelve shampoos, though they tend to last for a shorter, rather than a longer, time. They are often used to brighten up a natural colour rather than change it dramatically, and can give attractive highlights.

Finally there are permanent hair colours, which cannot be changed once done and are best done professionally in a salon. Some people are allergic to hair dyes, which is another good reason for not playing around with them at home. If you do decide to change your hair colour permanently, remember that the roots will need touching up every three or four weeks, which is a messy, as well as an expensive, business.

PERMING YOUR HAIR

Perming is also a drastic step to take, for, again, it has to grow out. It is an expensive operation, too, as it has to be done in a salon. It is not a good idea to experiment with home perms unless someone experienced can do it for you. Perms can give tight curls or just soft waves, and it is best to discuss with the hairdresser first what he or she thinks will be best for your hair.

HAIR ACCESSORIES

Nowadays you can buy a good assortment of hair slides and clips, combs and bands. As well as being pretty, they are useful aids to changing a hairstyle. You can pin back a fringe, sweep long hair up into a high, one-sided pony tail, or take all the hair away from your face and pin it up on top of your head. Hair bands can be made from ribbons and braids, or from elastic with badges, slides or buttons sewn or clipped on. If you want to look pretty and romantic you could wear a real flower in your hair, wired to a clip or slide. Hair that is long enough can be tied back with a scarf (the ends left trailing), or plaited, with beads woven in on a string. If you are lucky enough to have someone to help you, you could create wonderful beaded plaited styles, if your hair is long enough.

Experiment with different hair accessories. They don't cost very much and can change your whole appearance.

VISITING A HAIRDRESSER

Unless your hair is long and an obliging person can trim the ends for you, you will have to go to a hairdresser to get your hair cut and styled. Before you go, have a look through fashion magazines to see the kind of style you think you want, and take a picture of the style you decide on with you. Discuss it with the hairdresser. If he or she tells you the style you like won't work very well with your kind of hair it is best to listen to this advice, for otherwise you may pay a lot of money for a cut that doesn't suit you.

Although really original styles look great on special occasions, it may be as well to choose something simple that can just be washed, combed and left for every day, and dressed up for parties. The styles shown on the previous pages in this chapter are a good example. So have your hair cut into a good basic shape to start with, and then experiment. If you have nimble fingers you may be able to change your basic hairstyle to create lots of different effects. Very short hair needs little looking after, but regular trimming if it is to keep in shape, so bear that in mind. Also, there is not a lot that can be done to change its shape should you wish to do so. Long hair can be very adaptable, and needs cutting less often, but does take longer to wash and dry. As with all the other aspects of dress, fashion and appearance,

the choice is yours.

BEAVER BESTSELLERS

If you enjoyed this book, why not read some more of our bestselling Beaver books. You'll find thrilling stories, hilarious jokes and crazy poems for everyone to enjoy. They are available in bookshops or they can be ordered directly from us. Just complete the form below and send the right amount of money and the books will be sent to you at home.

☐ THE FOLK OF THE FARAWAY TREE	Enid Blyton	£1.75
☐ NICHOLAS AT LARGE	Goscinny and Sempé	95p
☐ EMIL AND HIS CLEVER PIG	Astrid Lindgren	95p
☐ REBECCA'S WORLD	Terry Nation	£1.50
☐ CONRAD	Christine Nostlinger	£1.50
☐ LITTLE OLD MRS PEPPERPOT	Alf Proysen	£1.25
☐ THE MIDNIGHT KITTENS	Dodie Smith	95p
☐ THE GREAT ICE-CREAM CRIME	Hazel Townson	£1.25
☐ BOGWOPPIT	Ursula Moray Williams	£1.75
☐ THE SIEGE OF WHITE DEER PARK	Colin Dann	£1.75
☐ THE WINTER VISITOR	Joan Lingard	£1.25
☐ SNOWY RIVER BRUMBY	Elyne Mitchell	£1.25
☐ BEOWULF	Robert Nye	£1.25
☐ GHOSTLY AND GHASTLY	Barbara Ireson (editor)	£1.50
☐ HOW TO HANDLE GROWN-UPS	Jim and Duncan Eldridge	£1.25
☐ HOW TO SURVIVE SCHOOL	Don Shiach	£1.50
☐ IT'S FUNNY WHEN YOU LOOK AT IT	Colin West	£1.25
☐ MAGIC TOYS, TRICKS AND ILLUSIONS	Eric Kenneway	£1.50
☐ MY FAVOURITE ANIMAL STORIES	Gerald Durrell	£1.95

If you would like to order books, please send this form, and the money due to:
ARROW BOOKS, BOOKSERVICE BY POST, PO BOX 29, DOUGLAS, ISLE OF MAN, BRITISH ISLES. Please enclose a cheque or postal order made out to Arrow Books Ltd for the amount due including 30p per book for postage and packing both for orders within the UK and for overseas orders.

NAME ....

ADDRESS ....

....

Please print clearly.